"YOU ARE *the* SALT *of the* EARTH…"
…*Confronting the Sin of our Silence!*

TED ROBERTS

© 2021 by Ted Roberts

All rights reserved solely by the author. The author guarantees all contents are original and do not infringe upon the legal rights of any other person or work. No part of this book may be reproduced in any form without the permission of the author. The views expressed in this book are not necessarily those of the publisher.

Due to the changing nature of the Internet, if there are any web addresses, links, or URLs included in this manuscript, these may have been altered and may no longer be accessible. The views and opinions shared in this book belong solely to the author and do not necessarily reflect those of the publisher. The publisher therefore disclaims responsibility for the views or opinions expressed within the work.

Unless otherwise indicated, Scripture quotations taken from the Holy Bible, New International Version (NIV). Copyright © 1973, 1978, 1984, 2011 by Biblica, Inc.™. Used by permission. All rights reserved.

Paperback ISBN-13: 978-1-6628-2545-3
Hard Cover ISBN-13: 978-1-6628-2546-0
Ebook ISBN-13: 978-1-6628-2547-7

BOOK DEDICATION

People are known to dedicate ships, buildings, monuments and their own accomplishments. The Bible says, "Give everyone what is due him; tribute to whom tribute is due, respect to whom respect is due, honor to whom honor is due" (Romans 13:7). I am dedicating this book as a tribute to Merle Moore, a living soul. Merle Moore is my brother in Christ. While on this earth Merle was a man of God, a man committed to prayer, a man who loved the Lord with all his heart and who delighted in His Word! It was Merles desire that others would come to know Jesus as their Lord and Savior as well. He was and is a man worthy of respect and honor!

Merle is now in the presence of the Lord whom he loved and served but his influence and the seeds he planted are still bearing fruit to this very day. His influence and his encouragement and his impact on my life cannot be overstated. I believe this book has in part come to fruition because of his love of the Word of God and his many prayers. Not only did Merle delight in doing the Lords work, but he also took pride in the physical work of his hands. Merle, what a joy and delight it must have been when you first heard these words from the lips of Jesus, "Well done, good and faithful servant! You have been faithful with a few things; I will put you in charge of many things. Come and share your master's happiness! (Matthew 25:21).

May those of us who are fellow Christ followers that knew and loved you while on your pilgrimage here on earth find comfort in the fact that we will see you again when we ourselves will be reunited with you in the Land of Glory!

ACKNOWLEDGEMENT PAGE

Jesus said, "Whoever acknowledges me before men, I will also acknowledge him before my Father in Heaven" (Matthew 10:32). The Apostle Paul acknowledged many who came alongside him in God's kingdom work. And Paul said, "Whatever you do, whether in word or deed, do it all in the name of our Lord Jesus, giving thanks to God the Father through him" (Colossians 3:17). Some of the things we do may seem trivial, but nothing is trivial when we do it for the glory of God.

Jesus asks us the question, "Are not five sparrows sold for two pennies?" And then he makes the statement, "Yet not one of them is forgotten by God" (Luke 12:6) and then he goes on to say, "Indeed, your very hairs are numbered." No, he will not forget the works we have done for his kingdom, he will acknowledge us, and he will acknowledge them.

I would like at this time to acknowledge a brother in Christ, Ron Scott, who has come along side my wife Sue and I, whom by his gifts of time, talents and financial support has helped us in the publishing of this book! His patience, his many hours of time and his computer expertise and financial support has made it possible for this book to be placed into your hands.

I would also like to acknowledge my wife Sue. Proverbs 18:22 says "The man who finds a wife finds a treasure and receives favor from the LORD." She has been by my side for over 28 years and when you read these poems you will see that at times that side has been a dark side, a not so pretty side at times. She is a person who shows unconditional love to all. God's grace has been poured out on me through her and I truly have received favor from the LORD. She is indeed a precious jewel, a treasure to me!

And I would also like to acknowledge another brother in Christ, my friend and prayer partner of many years, Everett Barker, who was there for me when I went through the darkest of valleys and listened to me during those times when I poured out the bitterness of my soul and he helped carry the weight of the burdens that I was not able to carry on my own (Galatians 6:2).

I am thankful for their patience and all the love and support they have shown me. It is their pictures that should be on the back of this book. And for all those that I have not acknowledged that have impacted and influenced me and supported me throughout the years, the Lord Himself will acknowledge them at some future time. My appreciation goes out to you all!

TABLE OF CONTENTS

Part I. Poems of Inspiration 1
  1. The Three Gardens 3
  2. Treasure Hunt 12
  3. The Soil 17
  4. Deception 26
  5. Have you ever Pondered the Heavens? 38
  6. The Disciples Prayer 44
  7. The Privileged Planet 55
  8. Heaven's Hope 59
  9. Hell: There really is such a Place 67
  10. Quest for Character 83
  11. If only I could Speak 91
  12. The Grandeur of God 112
  13. Satan's Goal 118
  14. Be Calm 131
  15. Depart from me, Lord, I am a sinful man 136
  16. You can be Sure 161
  17. Bugs and Things 185
  18. Suffering 189
  19. We too will Rise! 214
  20. What Won't be in Heaven 219
  21. God's Questions 222

Part II. Letters to the Editor **227**
  1. Bruised Reeds and Smoldering Wicks 229
  2. Are you in a Hurry? 231
  3. Questions to Ponder 233
  4. A Message of Hope 235
  5. A Religious World 237
  6. I used to be a fool 239
  7. Did God Really Say? 241
  8. Freedom of Speech 243
  9. Yes Dakota, the Christmas Story is a True
        Masterpiece 245
  10. Life is Precious 247
  11. Politics are Dirty? 249
  12. Political and Spiritual Character Assassination 251
  13. The Heart of the Christmas Story 253
  14. Politicians and their Craft 255
  15. The Sky is Falling!! 257
  16. The Plumb Line and the Pendulum 259
  17. Sex, Scandal and Sin 261
  18. Seed Planters 263
  19. Should not God's Voice be Heard Today? 265
  20. Socialism 267
  21. The Touch of Christmas 269
  22. Show tolerance—You sly guy 271
  23. What Difference does it Make!!!? 274
  24. Sex, who makes the Rules? 276
  25. Muddied Water's 278
  26. The Book 280
  27. The Heart of America 282
  28. If I were a Christian 284

About the Author **287**

Part One.

"YOU ARE *the* SALT *of the* EARTH…"

POEMS OF INSPIRATION

1. The Three Gardens

In the very first book of the Bible
We see that God made a very special place
He made a world that was meant to be inhabited
He prepared it for the human race
Isaiah 45:18

God prepared a paradise for Adam and Eve
Filled with beautiful plants and trees
A garden overflowing with His provision and benevolence
Free of pestilence and disease
Genesis 2

God had only one restriction in the Garden
Just one tree from which they could not eat
But there was a tempter in the Garden
Saying that the forbidden fruit was in fact tasty, very sweet
Genesis 2:17, 3:1

Temptations come in the form of a conversation
That takes place inside both me and you
Good choices or bad choices are always before us
A struggle between the two

God has given me a garden
He has given me a precious tree
But how often I have been surrounded by forbidden fruit
How often the enemy has tempted me
Proverbs 5:15-19

I wish that I could tell you
That not once had I tasted from the fruit
That permeated from the forbidden tree
That rose up from the poisonous root

But that would be far from truthful
Indeed, it would be an outright lie
Because I picked and then I tasted
After finding it to be pleasing to my eye

The Garden was a garden filled with beauty
All Eve needed was provided for
A perfect paradise filled with splendor
What made Eve to desire something more?

Satan is very subtle and very clever
And his strategy is to confuse reality
To make evil seem good and good seem evil
Have we not all tasted fruit from a forbidden tree?
Isaiah 5:20

'You must not eat from any tree in the garden'
Is that what God really said?
You see Satan had a plan and a strategy
He planted a seed of doubt inside Eve's head
Genesis 3:1

Adam and Eve were living in all the majesty of Eden
All they needed was provided for the two of them
But when they ate the forbidden fruit, the splendor was lost
Soon the deadly seeds from the tree would be carried
by the wind
Genesis 4:1-16

Eating from the forbidden tree had deadly consequences
And the forbidden tree had many deadly seeds
And today it is no longer a single forbidden tree
Paradise has been replaced with a garden full of deadly weeds

Eve's attention was focused on the single tree
It looked good and was pleasing to the eye
And it was also desirable for growing in wisdom
She fell for the devil's deceptive lie
Genesis 3:6

Satan whispered, the forbidden fruit is good for food
Why should you deny yourself such a treat?
Why should God keep you from what is delicious?
Whispering go ahead, take of the fruit and eat

What is it that God is afraid of?
That He would deny you such a pleasure
There are no barriers or fence around the tree
Besides, it is not as if it were a hidden treasure

Can you not smell the sweet aroma of its fruit?
The fruit is not out of your reach
Go ahead and pick one from the tree
It is more delicious than a Georgia peach

She forfeited the garden with its lavish provision
She put her focus on just one single tree
Satan gets her to concentrate on the temptation
How often has this happened to you and me?

Satan makes her aware of a restriction
Suggesting that God is keeping something good from her
Satan's deadly seed started to do its poisonous work
Causing her to doubt God's good character

This same temptation has been repeated and replayed
Again and again throughout history
The specifics are different, but the strategy is often the same
And the consequences always produce pain and misery

Eat from the life-giving trees in the garden!
Eat until you are satisfied and full
Although today there are many bad trees in this world's garden
Good trees are plenty and bountiful

What were the consequences of their disobedience?
First there was guilt and shame
And when they were confronted with their rebelliousness
The first thing they did was to cast the blame
Genesis 3:12-13

Instead of enjoying close intimate fellowship with God
The two of them tried to hide from God and His Holy presence
Another deadly seed produced as a result of their foolish choice
For one cannot hide from omnipresence
Genesis 3:10

When we listen to Satan's lies
Sin always exacts a heavy toll
Drudgery and difficulties will be our daily lot
The results weighing heavily on our soul

They were driven out of the beautiful Garden
And cast out into an unfriendly wilderness
Casting the blame instead of confession
Their peace was replaced with strain and stress
Genesis 3:23

It pleases God when we are honest
He does not want us to hide and conceal our sin
Satan wants us to turn our backs on God and walk the other way
But God wants us to freely come to Him
Matthew 11:28-30

Dirty dishes need to be washed and cleaned
The clothes we wear need laundering
Jesus wants us to keep moving toward the light
Satan wants to keep us in the dark and wandering

We do not say, why bother washing the dishes
They will just get dirty again
And we should not say, why bother confessing our sin
Cleansing comes when we confess our sin
John 13:10

Satan is the enemy of our soul
And he wants us to live in doubt and fear
He wants to keep us from moving forward
He wants us to keep looking in the rearview mirror

But our Heavenly Father wants us to keep moving forward
Even if it is just one small step at a time
He wants us to fix our eyes on Jesus
He wants us to renew our heart and renew our mind
Hebrews 12:2; Romans 12:2

At first, there were no thorns or thistles in the garden
There were no decaying trees
There was no poison oak or poison ivy
There was no poison oil on their leaves

Sin and seeds have a lot in common
Cannot many metaphors be found?
For example, take a single seed
That has been planted in the ground

It does not remain a single seed
It grows into a plant or into a tree
And if we allow sin to take root into our heart
It will grow and spread through you and me
John 12:24-25

Have you ever observed the seeds of a dandelion?
How easily they are carried by the wind
They do not remain stationary or in a single place
And the same is true of sin

That is why we need to plant godly seeds
For they also will spread and grow
And the Bible makes it very clear
That what we reap is what we sow
Galatians 6:7-9

In the Gospels we read of another Garden
Where the storm clouds had been gathering ominously
It was where Jesus began His passion
In the Garden of Gethsemane

Jesus was about to drink from the Cup of Agony
That even the movie "The Passion" could not convey
Jesus' physical, emotional, and spiritual agony in the garden
And the agony He would bear on the cross the following day

Death in its most dreadful appearances
Attended with all its terrors, looked Jesus in the face
Yet He accommodated himself to his undertaking
He would suffer for our sins and take our place

As the darkness loomed over him in the garden
He knew he would be drinking from the Cup of Suffering
He would drink the entire contents of the cup
He would experience death with its awful sting
I Corinthians 15:56

But the death He would experience
His death would not just be physical
For His death would carry all the sins of humanity
A cup of sins that was all-inclusive and full

Though He had a quick sense of the extreme bitterness
Of the suffering He would undergo
Yet He was willing to submit to them for our redemption
and salvation
For He knew the worth and value of a human soul

In His prayer He begs favor of His Father
If it is possible, let this cup pass from me
Only God could make provision for the cleansing of our sins
He did this by His incarnation and sharing in our humanity
Matthew 26:39; Philippians 2:6-11

His prayer was sorrowful and very heavy
What was it that put Him in this agony?
Certainly, it was nothing of despair or distrust of His Father
But that He was engaged in battle against the enemy
Luke 4:13

The sufferings He was entering upon were for our sins
Meditate on the hymn "Amazing Grace"
He would absorb the punishment of all not just for one
When on the cross He would take our place
John 3:16; I John 2:2

You are the Salt of the Earth

He had a clear prospect of all the sufferings that were before Him
The malice of the Jews and their base ingratitude
He foresaw the treachery of Judas, the unkindness of Peter
That "all" of us will stand before God someday is not a platitude

For God's Word makes it very clear
That each one of us is guilty of sin
All of us have eaten of the forbidden fruit
There is not a single exception
Romans 3:23

In Eden we see sins entrance in the Garden
We see the affects and consequences of the Fall
In the Garden of Gethsemane, we see God's provision
of cleansing
With an invitation of forgiveness offered to one and all
Matthew 11:28-30; Revelation 3:20

His was a painful and shameful death above any other
He was crucified at a place called Calvary
It was known as the place of the skull
A place famous for its disgrace and misery

Jesus was reviled and reproached by the people
And the religious rulers stood among the rabble
As they derided Him in their disdain and hatred
They encouraged and joined in with the meaningless gabble

They made a jest of His sufferings
As they stood among the unruly crowd
They joined in with those who were boisterous and disruptive
With those who were foul-mouthed, belligerent and loud

Jesus voluntarily chose to go to the cross
He willingly did it on our behalf
And now you too have a choice to make
Will you join in with those who mock and laugh?

Or will you humble yourself before Him
And grasp the real meaning of the cross
Will you give ear to Jesus' invitation?
His desire is that no one will be loss
II Peter 3:9

For He desires your presence in the New Kingdom
He wants you to spend eternity in this beautiful place
Will you repent and acknowledge your sin?
Will you accept His provision of grace?
Luke 14:15-24; Matthew 18:3

Because He is preparing another Garden
Please come with me and take a look
For you will find it in the last chapters of the Bible
The climactic finish of His Holy Book

As we look at this Garden that is to come
A New World now opens to our view
A New Garden where no deadly seeds are permitted
An Eternal Garden where everything will be made new
Revelation 21:1-5

Heaven can be described as a Garden, a Paradise if you will
As Christians, we should be looking forward to the day
Where there will be no more death, corruption or sorrow
The day all our tears shall be wiped away

The heavenly state is here described as a Paradise
A paradise in a heavenly city
A large and permanent heavenly settlement
Not a private or individual municipality

Let the seeds of God's Word take root in your heart and be a beautiful blossom in God's Garden, firmly rooted in the courtyard of God!

2. Treasure Hunt

Our children love being read to
Being read to is a very special gift
Sadly, it is a gift that is often neglected
Having been cast aside and set adrift

Children enjoy exciting stories
Stories of courage and bravery
Stories of pirates battling on the high seas
Suspenseful stories filled with mysteries

Reading stories create a special time of bonding
Between a parent and a child
When was the last time you read a story to your children?
Has it been a little while?

Some people search for sunken treasures
Treasures that lie deep beneath the sea
Some observe the heavens in the night sky
Hoping to make a new discovery

But a good story is truly a treasure
Stimulating the imagination of a child's mind
A helpful tool in a child's development
A good investment in our use of time

God's universe is filled with wonders
So is our home that we call earth
And what about the wonder of Emanuel
And the mystery of the Virgin Birth
Matthew 1:22-23; Isaiah 7:14

Ah, and nature itself is filled with wonders
And in a child's heart there is a yearning
There await many discoveries to be uncovered
I plead you unwrap their God-given gift of learning
Romans 1:20; II Peter 1:5

Do we not as adults have a tendency
To lose our sense of wonder?
Maybe we are in need of redirecting our focus
And once again stand in awe of God's majestic thunder
Psalm 19

Sometimes it is easy to focus on all the problems
After all, this world is a dark and dismal place
Wars, crime, diseases, and corruption
A world in need of God's mercy and His grace

Some say, surely there is no room for joy and laughter
In such a dark world with unending needs
No room to look upon and enjoy "the lilies of the field"
Or to ponder on the miracles of seeds
Luke 12:27; Mark 4:26-29

Some say, do you not realize the sky is falling
The world is in turmoil and distress
We must be busy about the Kings business
How can one find tranquility and rest?
Matthew 14:23; Luke 19:13; Matthew 11:28-30

As adults we who call ourselves Christians
We are called by God to come aside
To be still and not overburdened
And in Christ we are called to abide
Mark 6:31; John 15:7

We ourselves need to hear the words of Jesus
Open our Bibles like those who sat at Jesus' feet
They listened to the One who came to redeem us
The One who desires to restore us and make us complete
Luke 10:39

Jesus spoke to the people in parables
Spoke of eternity, heaven and of hell
Spoke of the love of the Father
There were so many wonderful stories He had to tell
Matthew 13:3; 1st John 3:1

And Jesus spoke of the wonders of nature
Spoke of the mystery of the seed
Spoke of the master of deception
And warned us to beware of the deadly weed
Mark 4:26-29; John 8:44; Matthew 13:24-43

Jesus' stories were filled with deep meaning
Impregnated with the Father's truth
And the book of Proverbs is the book of wisdom
Teaching us adults how we are to train up our youth

And the true stories in the Old Testament
Today they seem to be misplaced and out of season
But "all Scripture is God-breathed and is useful for teaching"
God has placed them there for a reason
Luke 24:25-27; II Timothy 3:4; II Timothy 3:16

Stories can stir our imagination
Transport us to a different place and time
All the true stories we find in the Bible
Are there to help us in the renewing of our mind
Romans 12:2

Peter, under the inspiration of the Holy Spirit
Clearly expounded on this truth
Speaking of teachers who would exploit our children
To try to steal away the hearts of our youth

Our stories should challenge our children
They should stimulate them to wholesome thinking
Because the stories that our culture is teaching
Are placing them on a doomed ship that is slowly sinking

The stories we read to our children
Should stimulate Christian growth and character
To help replace cowardliness with courage
Fill their spirit with moral quality and fiber
II Peter 1:5-9

The Bible often warns of false prophets
Of those who would attempt to lead us and our children astray
Of those who masquerade themselves as angels of light
Indeed, there are many of them out there today
Matthew 7:15; II Corinthians 11:14; II Peter 2:1

Peter said, in the last days there will be stories written
by scoffers
By those who are willingly ignorant of the truth
That is why it is important we teach our children
And ground them in God's Word while in their youth
II Peter 3:5; Colossians 2:7

You are the Salt of the Earth

We must not underestimate the shrewdness of false teachers
And we ourselves must be astute and alert
For if we neglect the true stories in the Bible
It will be the cause of our downfall and our hurt

Unlike the teachers of the Law
Jesus spoke with authority and was direct
Should we not as Christians embrace his teachings?
Approach them with reverence and respect
Matthew 7:28-29; John 6:63

Is our enemy's strategy without rhyme and reason?
No, our enemy has a purpose with design
He is not ignorant but beguiling and deceptive
He indeed has a reason and rhyme

The enemy's methods are used like lures that are attractive
He often uses means of trickery
Leading our children down a slippery slope
While hiding behind a mask of dishonesty

So, set aside some time to read uplifting stories
Take your children on a treasure hunt so to speak
And start them on a lifelong adventure
So that they too will learn to ask, knock and seek
Luke 11:9

Make it a habit to read to your children
Make it a top priority
It will stimulate them to wholesome thinking
It will be a key to help unlock life's mystery
Proverbs Chapter 2

Written for the Glory of God

3. The Soil

Jesus often spoke in parables
You will find them in the Word of God
His first is preeminently important
As it speaks of the soil and the sod
Matthew 13:1-23; Mark: 4:1-20; Luke 8:4-15

Parables are written for true believers
For those who really want to understand
For those who have a spiritual thirst and hunger
In a spiritual dry and barren land
Matthew 13:15; Matthew 5:5; Isaiah 9:2; Luke 1:79

At times Jesus spoke of birds symbolically
Sometimes to illustrate a particular truth
We should use Jesus' parables today in our churches
As a means of educating both adults and youth
Matthew 13:4

In the parable of the Sower
We are challenged to examine ourselves
It is wise for us to do this from time to time
And not leave our Bibles unopened on our shelves
II Corinthians 13:5; II Peter 1:10-11

You are the Salt of the Earth

Jesus spoke a lot about a person's character
And about personal responsibility
Is your Bible covered with dust and cobwebs?
Is God's Word fulfilling its intended purpose for you and me?
Matthew 25:14-30; James 1:22-25

We see this promise throughout the Bible
Of spiritual fruit from spiritual seed
Jesus wants us to be deep rooted
Our Heavenly Father wants us to succeed
Galatians 6:7; Colossians 2:6-7; Matthew 25:23

Are you just a churchgoer…a religious person?
One who goes to church week after week?
Or are you one who loves Jesus and his teaching
With the desire to ask and knock and seek
James 1:22-25; John 14:21; Matthew 7:7-8

Are you going to church just out of duty?
You say, well, at least I am going to church
Be careful, that could turn you into a good Pharisee
Week after week sitting on your perch

Parables are illustrative stories
That Jesus has given you and me
Are you a follower of Jesus?
Do you have the ears to hear and eyes to see?
Luke 10:41-42

Jesus was often surrounded by great crowds
But not all liked what he had to say
Some had ears but chose not to listen
While others fought to keep His words at bay
Matthew 13:32; Mark 4:23; Isaiah 29:13; Matthew 15:8

In the parable of the Sower
There was no difference in the seed
It was the responsibility and resolve of the soil
That would determine whether it would succeed
Luke 8:11

Jesus compared human hearts to different soils
In this very illustrative story
The good soil fulfills its God intended purpose
To bring forth good fruit and bring God glory
Matthew 13:8; 1st Corinthians 10:31

The heart of a true learner
Is like rich soil in a field
Tended by a farmer with a purpose
Together they will produce a fruitful yield

Do you have that kind of heart?
Do you have a heart with a willingness to learn?
Do you have a hunger and thirst for the things of God?
Do you have the ability to discern?
Luke 10:41-42; Matthew 5:6

The person who can learn but doesn't
Is one who chooses not to hear
Can such a one be called a Christian?
But blessed are those who hear and then draw near
James 4:8

Again, the heart of a true learner
Is like rich soil in a field
And at the end of the growing season
There will be a harvest and a yield
Galatians 6:10

First, are our ears attentive to the Word of God?
Do we have a desire deep within?
To be more Christlike in our character
Do we have a longing to be more like him?
Matthew 4:4; John 6:63; II Peter 1:5-10

Are the seeds of godly character
Taking root within your heart?
Sometimes the growth may seem imperceptible
But has the seed even had an opportunity to start?

The adventure of learning is before us
Let us follow along the lighted trail
Let us walk the path that God has set before us
Let the wind of His Spirit catch our sail
Psalm 119:105; 1st John 1:7

The kind of soil you choose to be
Is determined by freewill and your own choice
As to whether your ears are willingly opened
To listen to and be drawn to the Savior's voice
Luke 9:35; John 6:44

Sadly, many choose to listen to the deceiver
Many choose this world's temporary pleasures
Many turn their back on Jesus and his teachings
And on Heaven with all its eternal treasures
Matthew 7:3-3; Matthew 16:26; Matthew 6:19-20

Sometimes growth comes in spurts
Sometimes growth is affected for different reasons
The amount of rain and sunshine affects the soil
Sometimes growth may be stunted through the winter seasons

Sometimes the sun and heat are relentless
Other times there may be torrents of rain
Sometimes the crops are battered by the wind
Yet at harvest time there will still be a crop of grain
Matthew 7:24-27; Matthew 13:8

Good soil allows the seed to germinate
It allows the seed to birth
It allows the farmer to have his way
Allows the roots to go down deep beneath the earth
Colossians 2:7

Jesus spoke of four different kinds of soil
Jesus said we are to ask and knock and search
This should be taking place each day of the week
Not just on Sunday morning in our church
Matthew 7:7; Matthew 6:11

This parable is of preeminent importance
It is where we each should start
We should ask ourselves, are we cultivating biblical principles?
Do we have a pliable teachable heart?

Or has your heart turned hard and cold
Has the root of bitterness settled in?
Have the weeds overtaken your garden?
You no longer look to Him
Proverbs 24:33-34

Do you have a love relationship with the Heavenly Father?
A desire to walk in His holy light
No one will ever attain perfection in this flesh
But there should be a desire to do what is right
Luke 10:27; 1st John 1:7; John 5:28-29

The good seed is the Word of God
The four soils speak of the human heart
Do you have the ears to hear, is your heart receptive?
To the wisdom God wants to impart
John 8:11

The etymology of the word disciple may be helpful
Disciple comes from the Latin word discern
Think of pupil, student, and follower
One with a willingness in his heart to learn

For one who professes to be a Christian
Being a lifelong learner should be our goal
Learning makes a man fit company for his fellow man
It is letting God's Word be deep rooted in one's soul

Are you open to counsel and correction?
Will you allow for a little pruning to take place?
As a Christian it is necessary
If you are to grow in God's wisdom and His grace
Proverbs 27:12; John 15:1-2; II Peter 3:18

Sadly, sometimes we play the fool
And choose to do what is right in our own eyes
As fools we stubbornly set our own course
Leading to our own downfall and demise

Although one may not immediately die physically
Although death may not come until a future day
One's sensitivity to God's Spirit may slowly die
If one continues to travel the path of his own way
Acts chapter 26

Someone can expose us to the truth
But he cannot make us learn
Sadly, many choose the wide gate and the broad road
And the truth of God they choose to spurn
Matthew 7:13

Ask yourself, what kind of soil am I?
You know there will be a Judgment Day
If you want to escape the judgment
Well, Jesus has made for all a way

Prayerfully read John's Gospel
And all the claims of Jesus Christ
He speaks of our need of a spiritual birth
And his claim to be the way the truth the life
John 6:35, 8:12, 10:9, 10:11, 11:25, 14:6, 15:1; John Chapter 3; John 14:6

Do a little self evaluation
Take a serious look within
Come to grips with the inescapability of death
Acknowledge the reality of your own sin
II Corinthians 13:5; Hebrews 9:27

If you have been in church for ten years
In a solid biblical church
In a church that correctly handles the truth
If you have been attentive as you perch

Then you should have a basic understanding
Of what it means to be born again
And of what Christ did on the cross on your behalf
To cleanse you of your sin
John 3:3; 1st Peter 3:18

The reason for learning for the Christian
Is to bring us into line
With God's purposes and His values
And the renewing of our mind
II Peter 1:5-9; Romans 12:1-2

Knowing God's will in a confusing world
Is never an easy task
As Christians we are to grow in God's wisdom
We are to knock and seek and ask
II Peter 3:18; Matthew 7:7

We must be always attentive
And understand our responsibility
Be good stewards of the talents entrusted to us
God's Word often speaks of accountability
Matthew 25:14-30; Philippians 2:1-11

One's attitude is very important
One needs to consider the claims of Christ
One needs to understand free will and volition…
And from time to time take inventory of one's own life
John 6:35; 8:12; 10:7; 10:11; 11:25; 14:6; 15:1
Joshua 24:14-15; I Timothy 2:4; II Corinthians 13:5; II Peter 1:10

The heart is the soil of which Jesus speaks
The nucleus of our learning center
For there to be a fruitful harvest
The soil needs to allow the seed to enter

This requires our ears to be open
And to observe well with our eyes
And to meditate on the Word of God
To help us to distinguish truth from lies
Matthew 11:15; Psalm 1

Are you being challenged by the Word of God?
Are you keeping eternity in view?
Is your faith growing through life's challenges?
Will the words "well done" be said to you?
Ecclesiastes 3:11; James 1;2; I Peter 1:6; Matthew 25:23

Jesus told the people many parables
Jesus' parables are like rich pearls full of truth
Seeds to be planted in our children's hearts
While young and in their youth
*Mark 12:2; Matthew 13:3; Deuteronomy 6:4-9; Matthew 19:14;
Proverbs 22:6*

If we want our children to be successful learners
And shouldn't that be our goal?
We may need to reprioritize our time and efforts
And make an investment in their soul
Deuteronomy 6:6

The end of learning is to know God
Learning to know God should be our end
And out of that knowledge to love Him with all our heart
Our goal should bring honor onto Him

So be good soil in God's garden
Receive His seed into your heart
Let God's Word dwell in you richly and be fruitful
God calls us to be holy and set apart
Colossians 3:16; Galatians 5:22-23; I Peter 3:15; II Corinthians 6:17

Written for the Glory of God

4. Deception

Lies, deceit and deception
Sham and treachery
False pretense, corruption and cheating
Betrayal and trickery

Fake, phony and counterfeit
Imitation and mimicry
Impersonations and false impressions
Half-truths and dishonesty

The amazing octopus is astounding
It is an incredible master of disguise
It can instantly blend in with its surroundings
And vanish before your very eyes

Some animals and insects are defenseless
And would be unable to survive
Had their Creator not provided them with camouflage
That enables them to stay alive

At first, everything that God created was very good
But when man chose to sin it was followed by a dreadful curse
Not only did sin bring death to humanity
Sin would affect the entire universe
Genesis 3:17-19; Romans 8:18-25

God's creative genius is so often overlooked
But still His Creation tells an awesome story
Even beyond the destructiveness of death and decay
caused by sin
All that is good still brings the God of Heaven glory

The animal kingdom is a dangerous world
Often, it is a world of hide and seek
There are large and vicious animals
And there are some who are small and very weak

You have heard the expression "The survival of the fittest"
But in the world of camouflage this is not true
It is a world of fascinating deception
And the amazing things that animals do

Animals use disguises to protect themselves
Enabling them to survive another day
Enabling to hide from predators in plain sight
And they do this in such a spectacular way

Without actually being invisible
Without actually being out of sight
They use trickery to escape their enemy
Without putting up a fight

Sometimes the masquerade seems to be anything but camouflage
Sometimes mimicry is the method that is used
Some want their shapes and bright colors to be seen
Causing their enemies to be confused

The amazing lacewing larva
Creatively builds its own camouflage
From materials it finds in its own home environment
Like an artist creating a colorful collage

Animals are "designed" to use various methods
To make themselves less noticeable
God is the Master genius behind every design
Evolutionary theories are filled with a multitude of holes

Some animals have colors to match their surroundings
Some can ingeniously change their color to blend in
It is God who gave them this resourceful talent
The ability to change the color of their skin

Nature is filled with many miraculous wonders
Revealing God's ingenuity
Strange differences of diversification
Impersonators with the art of mimicry

Praying mantis that blend in perfectly
Katydids that mimic leaves
Hornworms with stripes that looks like veins of a leaf
Owls "whooooooo" blend in with the bark of trees

And some katydids mimic dangerous wasps
Let us take the time to think this through
Millions of mutations over billions of years
Do you really believe such silliness is true?

Who does the selecting in natural selection anyway?
I think it is time that we get real
When someone lies and tries to trick you
How does that make you feel?

People are far superior to the animals
People are able to reason and articulate
But because of their sinful nature
They are capable of being filled with cruel hate

Do plants and flowers reason and articulate?
Plants and flowers are not able to think
It is God who created these useful and beautiful flowers
Otherwise, they would not exist they would be extinct

God is the God of the spectacular
All one need do is look at the katydids
God is the God of what appears to be the mundane
All one need do is look at the caterpillars that look like twigs

As we can see when we study nature
Creatures have a large variety in their bag of tricks
Birds that talk and birds that mimic
And maybe you have seen some of the amazing walking sticks

Evolutionists act as if mutations
Are capable of intelligence
That they have eyes and can see their surroundings
But that does not make any sense

Tree hoppers that look like thorns
Caterpillars with a clever disguise
Some that look just like bird droppings
Some look like snakes that have big eyes

There is a great food chain in nature
It is a land filled with enemies
Army ants, scorpions and poisonous spiders
Venomous snakes and killer bees

Deception is the most important part
In natures game of mimicry
It is a land filled with con artists
A land of impersonation and trickery

When one looks at all of God's creativity in nature
One cannot help but note the perfection of mimicry
And that God is the great architect of the universe
The great God of design and symmetry

Warning signs and advertisements
Come through the eye gate and then enter the mind
By way of different colors, shapes and sizes
Even in this fallen world you can see design

How could a particular frog have any idea
That it has a pair of false eyes on its back
And lift up its rear to look more aggressive
To fend off an attack?
Cuyaba dwarf frog

My prayer is that the church would wake up
I pray that they would open up their eyes
And teach so that our children would have discernment
And that we would no longer believe the devil's lies

Mimicry is a complex form of deception
Rain forests are filled with leaf-imitating creatures
Looking like a fresh unblemished leaf
With their shape and color-matching features

As we can see there is camouflage throughout nature
But there is also camouflage in the heart of men
At times, the base nature of men is worse than animals
This nature is described in the Bible as sin
II Peter 2:12; Jude 1:10

Lies, deceit and deception
Sham and treachery
False pretense, corruption and cheating
Betrayal and trickery

Fake, phony and counterfeit
Imitation and mimicry
Impersonations and false impressions
Half-truths and dishonesty

Lawyer's fighting it out in the courtrooms
Siblings with hate in their heart toward their brother
Breakups in marriages and dysfunctional families
Brothers at war with one another

The eye of the hunter is keen
The hunters accomplish their tasks with skill
As they come out of their secret hiding place
As they move in for the kill

You have heard the expression "A wolf in sheep's clothing"
Yes, there are religious people who hide behind a façade
They try to sham and fleece the flock
And they do it in the name of God

The world is like a jungle filled with predators
All one need do is glimpse at fallen humanity
We clearly see the depravity of the human heart
We start to see ever increasing insanity

In the life of the jungle it is an eat or be eaten world
In the animal world it is not because of hate
For meat eating animals it is a matter of survival
And many patiently lie in wait

At times, the enemy's tactics can be subtle
Camouflaged and well disguised
Attacking us when we are at our weakest and most vulnerable
Often mixing truth in with their lies
II Corinthians 11:4, 14

Animals are born with instinct
That in and of itself is an amazing God-given ability
We need to remove the deceptive camouflage from
before our eyes
And use our spiritual eyes to see

Fraud and deception
Bribery and seduction
Temptation and allurement
Enticement and corruption

Hoax and schemes and scams
They plot with purpose and design
We need to continually put on God's armor
In the battle for our heart and mind
Ephesians 6:10-20

Some of these insects look like aliens from outer space
Like some strange and bizarre creatures
Some look exquisite and extraordinary
With their odd shape and bizarre features

Look at the words and terms in evolutionist writings
Look at the different words and you will find
Such words as talent-strategy-tactic-pretend-technique
and ingenious
And how many times you find the word design

As they describe all the incredible creatures of Creation
They use words that describe intelligence
To say unintelligent mutations brought about all the miraculous complexity
Is simply to embrace willful ignorance
II Peter 3:5

When we look at Genesis, the Book of beginnings
We see in print the first recorded lie
Coming straight from the prince of darkness
From the one who said "you will not surely die"
Genesis 3:4

Yet the world we live in is filled with death
And today multitudes still believe the lie
The same lie that was believed by our first parents
The question we need to ask ourselves "is why"

When children steal cookies from the cookie jar
It gives us as parents the opportunity to teach
But when big lies are being spoken by our culture
God calls those behind the pulpit to stand for the truth and preach
II Timothy 3:16-17; James 3:1

Today we see in psychological literature
Of people who play a deceitful game
Those who do bad or destructive things
But on others shift the blame

Freud coined a term about this phenomenon
Psychologists call this phenomenon "transference"
The devil is a master at deception
We need to beware of his false appearance
II Corinthians 11:14

Transference is obviously a form of lying
In its wrongful assignment of blame and responsibility
People no longer being held accountable for their bad behavior
As deception continues to permeate our society

This world with sinful people is a dangerous world
Do we not as people play hide and seek?
A destructive game of deceit and exploitation
Where the strong often take advantage of the vulnerable and weak
Romans 3:23; Genesis 3:8; Exodus 22:22-24

Perpetrators shift the blame of their bad behavior on the innocent
They say that their own bad behavior is good
Those who stand for the truth become their enemies
At the same time saying that they themselves are so misunderstood
Isaiah 5:20

How sad that so many professing Christians today
Have been duped by so many of our culture's lies
That they are so ill-equipped and unprepared
As they continue to build on a foundation of compromise
Hebrews 5:12

There are many who set in our churches today
They need to look up the word nominal
And those who teach should give the definition of facade
While in the pews they overflow

Hitler propagated a horrendous lie
"Transference" was the tool he used
Saying he and the Germans were the victims
While all the time the Jews were the victims he abused

He accused the Jews of being capitalists while at the same time
being Bolsheviks
From being impotent to lusting after Nordic woman
Of being culturally insignificant to being seekers of world
domination
The very sins ascribed to him

Should Christians be involved in politics?
On this topic what did Jesus have to say?
If we are to be salt and light in a decaying world
What does this question mean to us today?
Matthew 5:13

Of course, Christians should be involved in the
political process!
We must take a stand for integrity and righteousness
In a nation that continues to slide into moral depravity
Lest we be overcome and silenced by paralysis

For "evil prevails when good men do nothing"
But what can we as Christians do?
Maybe it is time we examined ourselves in light of Scripture
To see what Jesus expects of me and you

Maybe we Christians are not as good as we think we are
Maybe we love the things of this world a bit too much
Maybe we have misplaced our priorities in this life
And with the reality of eternity have lost touch

As Christians we are to fix our eyes on Jesus
Eternity should change the way we think
Much of the so-called church in America is like a ship
Taking on water and about to sink
Hebrews 12:2

As Christians we are to be in the world but not of it
We are to be Christ-like and unique
We are supposed to set our hearts and minds on things above
We are not to be caught up in emotionalism but to think
1st Corinthians 5:9-10; Romans 13:14; Colossians 3:1

Cultural lies have subtlety permeated the church
Relationship with Christ has been replaced with a religious façade
As a result, the church has become more worldly
Many no longer seeking after the mind of God

Before a Christian can be salt and light in society
They themselves have to be salt and light
The Bible says that judgment begins in the house of God
Today's church needs to get its priority right
Matthew 5:13-14; Mark 9:50; 1st Peter 4:17

How can one believe the lie that killing innocent children?
Is not a horrendous sin
How can one believe in the lie of evolution?
These deadly lies are like seeds being carried by the wind

There are many churches filled with superficial believers
I plead with you to open up the Word of God
It speaks of those who have a "dead" or "useless" faith
Those that could be called nominal Christians hiding behind a façade
Matthew 25:1-13; James 2:20

Read Jesus' Parable of the Sower
He says, "He who has ears to hear, let him hear"
Do not stand on the "soapbox" of self-righteousness
God's Word reveals our true character like a mirror
Matthew 13:1-23; James 1:22-25

A strong faith in a flimsy and easily broken plank
Could be the death of you
When trying to get to the other side of a raging river
But a weak faith in a strong plank will carry you through

Many true believers struggle with doubt from time to time
There are many who struggle with doubts who are true believers
That is why we should constantly have the truth placed before us
Lest we be outwitted by the deceivers

Written for the glory of God

5. Have You Ever Pondered the Heavens?

Have you ever wondered about the night sky?
On a clear and cloudless night?
While the air was crisp, and all was silent
And the stars glimmered crystal clear and bright
Psalm 8

Have you ever enjoyed an evening sunset?
Have you been delighted by the view?
As the colors merged together
Accentuated by a gentle blue
James 1:17

Have you ever seen a crescent moon?
Or an eclipse of the sun?
Or a shower of meteorites as you gazed up at a night sky?
As they appear in a blaze of glory one by one

Have you ever seen the Aurora Arboreal?
Known to many as the Northern Lights
A luminous phenomenon of colorful luminosity
Seen in the northern heavens of the night

A lustrous rainbow of colors in the night above us
Colors dancing freely in the sky
A work of living art that God has giving us
Majestic and pleasing to one's mind and eye

Have you ever seen in the early morning?
A beautiful sunrise
A lovely pastel of pink and blue on the horizon
An awe-inspiring painting that God has placed before
our very eyes

Have you ever pondered the miracle of birth?
You know it truly is a miracle
A miraculous journey from its beginning
The works of God are wonderful
Psalm 139

God speaks to those who are willing to listen
But sadly, many have no such desire
They refuse to open their ears and hearts to His majestic
providence
They make no effort to search for truth or to inquire
Isaiah 1:18; Matthew 13:15

Our Father desires to draw them
The One who created their very soul
But they continue to resist Him
The very One who longs to make them whole
John 6:44

Did you know the sun that shines so brightly?
It is itself a star
A star so much closer than the one's we see at night
The nighttime stars that are so distant and so far

Again, have you ever pondered the heavens?
Or the vastness of outer space?
The planets, moons and stars
And on the One who set them in their place?
Genesis 1:1; Isaiah 40:26

You would think that the great thinkers of our day
Would be humbled as they observe God's universe
That they would stand in awe of its Creator
As they contemplate it from this earth
Psalm 8; Psalm 19

But sadly, just the opposite is true
An arrogance that is rather odd
Being blinded by their worldly wisdom
They will not acknowledge God
I Corinthians 3:18-23; Psalm 14:1

Do you consider yourself to be a thinking person?
Able to distinguish fabrication from reality?
In a world full of fraud and deception
Are you able to distinguish truth from fantasy?
Matthew 22:37

We do not fail to acknowledge the great artists
For the masterpieces of work that they have done
Or the architects for their great structures
That have withstood centuries beneath the blazing sun

Evolutionists say, but ah! There is no need for God
You ask, where then do they put their faith and reliance?
Well, they are not such great thinkers after all
They replace the Creator with the god of so-called science

For much of what they call science
Is simply abstract fantasy
The truth is nonexistent in many of their theories
But a cloudy haze of absurdity

Evolutionary theory itself
Is based on the assumption of atheism
They say that God does not exist
For they want nothing to do with Him

Evolutionists claim that everything in the universe
Has accidentally evolved
From dead inanimate matter
In their blindness this is their conclusion, their resolve

And where did their imaginary matter come from?
What is their ultimate conclusion?
Well, that it arose from absolutely nothing
They have believed a lie, a deceptive deadly illusion

The theory of evolution
Provides the only other possible alternative
To explain how everything came into existence
All the amazing complexity of biological life that exists

The fundamental importance of this topic
Demands that we examine the mounting evidence
Showing that evolution is about to collapse under its
own weight
Scientifically it does not make any sense

When someone comes knocking at your door
It is usually somebody that you know
Or sometimes it may be a salesman wanting to get a foot inside
And you are quick to tell him no

Maybe you have come to the realization that God is real
You now believe that God exists
After pondering on the overwhelming evidence
You now know that God is not a myth

You ask, but now what do I do?
May I suggest that you open up God's Word
And listen to the words of Jesus
For that is where the Gospel can be heard

Jesus says, "Here I am! I stand at the door and knock"
If anyone hears my voice
And opens the door I will come in and eat with him
So, I ask, what will be your choice?
Revelation 3:20

God will not force Himself upon you
But maybe you hear Him knocking on your heart's door
Maybe you hear the voice of Jesus clearly speaking
I pray that you will not resist Him anymore
Acts 7:51

In the past have you shut up your door against Him?
That is what by nature sinners do
But he does not immediately withdraw his invitation
He is still graciously offering it to you

The evolutionists believe in a theory
That life rose out of a prebiotic soup
But their theory has a disgusting putrid smell
More than a cesspool full of filth and smelly poop

The evolutionary theory is fatally flawed
Every single step along the way
Empirical science reveals the reflected light of our Creator
And we keep finding more evidence every day

All living biological organisms are incredibly complex
Even the simplest one-celled bacterial organism
In which we discover an almost unbelievable miniature design
That could only come from Him

The Bible declares that God created
Each of the many species after its own kind
Which is exactly what the fossil record confirms
Which is exactly what we find

Handwriting can only come through an intelligent source
Take the time to think it through
And the Bible is a miraculous book of revelation
It is God's handwritten letter to me and you

But we also see His handwriting throughout nature
Especially in the incredible DNA
Something that Darwin knew nothing about
But evidence for intelligent design is overwhelming today

Written for the Glory of God

6. The Disciple's Prayer?

Jesus presented a model prayer for his disciples to follow
It is known as "the Lord's Prayer" today
But after some prayer and a little study
We might look at it in a different way

Might it not appropriately be called the "Disciple's prayer"
A model prayer for all Christians too
Containing elements that are important for all praying
For me as well you

When we look at some of the other teachings of Jesus on prayer
When we dive a little deeper in the Scripture
We see that Jesus leads us by example
That He paints for us a clear and vibrant picture
Ephesians 5:1

A picture of what it means to be a man of prayer
What it means to walk in true humility
What it means to depend on our Heavenly Father
An example to His disciples and you and me

Poems Of Inspiration

The Bible speaks a lot on prayer
Psalms one hundred speaks of the God who gives us life
That we should enter His gates with thanksgiving
And obviously we should give thanks to Jesus for his personal sacrifice
Psalm100:4-5

The Scriptures say that we should pray for one another
That we should ask and knock and seek
And if someone in our church body is suffering
That we should pray for those who are vulnerable and weak
James 5:16; Matthew 7:7

The disciple's prayer life reminds us to be holy
And that God is worthy of our trust
That our eyes should not be fixed on earthly pleasures
And not to store up treasures here on earth where things fade away and rust
Matthew 6:19-21

Biblically, there is nothing wrong with pleasure
There is nothing wrong with having things that are nice
But the Bible stresses balance
We need to beware of greed and vice
I Timothy 6:17; Proverbs 30:7-9

That we should trust God for our daily needs
"Give us today our daily bread"
That we would be a people who embrace forgiveness
That at night He would give us rest for our weary head
Matthew 6:11,12

The Lord's prayer is not so much a formula to be repeated
As it is a revelation of the attitude
With which we approach God as our Heavenly Father
We should approach Him with awe and gratitude

Like a young child who is loved by his daddy
A child who has complete confidence in his "Father-love"
Is how we should draw near the God of Heaven
Our loving Father in Heaven enthroned above

But Jesus said that in order to know God as our Heavenly Father
We first must be "born again"
We must understand the purpose of the cross
And we must understand our fallen state and the darkness
of our sin
John 3:1-21; Isaiah 59:2

We must understand His offer of forgiveness
And understand His mercy and His grace
We must understand what it means to have a broken contrite heart
Before we can enter in the "secret" place
II Corinthians 6:1-2; Isaiah 57:17

Maybe you never had a caring earthly father
Maybe you experienced from him sexual or physical abuse
Or maybe he was angry and verbally abusive
Leaving you bewildered and confused

Or maybe you grew up in an unloving foster home
Or had a stepfather who was cruel and mean
Or you were told that you would never amount to anything
Leaving you feel dirty and unclean

Or maybe your earthly father abandoned you
Just as he has rejected God above
He never held you in his arms and said "I love you"
He never showered you with a father's love

Poems Of Inspiration

But the God of Heaven is different than our earthly father
He walks with us even through the valley of the shadow of death
And Jesus said "come to me all you who are weary
And I will give you peace and rest"
Psalm 23; Matthew 11:28-30

Have you ever felt the spirit of adoption by a loving Father?
If not, there is nothing like it beneath the sky
To be part of the family of the living God
To be the apple of his eye
Ephesians 3:20

God's offer to all is to be part of His family
We can receive the Spirit of sonship if His offer we receive
A special kinship with the Heavenly Father
All He asks is that we repent of our sin and believe

The underlying word for sonship is "adoption"
Christians are adopted sons and daughters into God's
family by grace
Though now we see but a poor reflection
One day we shall see Him face to face
Romans 8:15; I Corinthians 13:12

If we desire to be adopted in His family
If we graciously accept His gift
If we allow Him to put His arms around us
We will see that He desires to encourage us and uplift

Then we will not be afraid that He will misunderstand us
If we put our words a little out of place
If our prayer is full of faults or even a foolish prayer
Because our Father wants to hold us tight in His embrace

Because He is unlike any earthly father
So much different than those we see throughout our land today
He is far superior to even the best of fathers
For He is perfect in every way

He is also better than any father-in-law
Even if your father-in-law is a godly man
Those who try to do their very best
And there are many scattered throughout our great land

Let us draw near to His throne as children
For He understands our weaknesses and our fears
In our secret place we can reveal to Him our frailties
We can come to Him unashamedly with our tears
Hebrews 10:22

Knowing God in an intimate and private way
Will free us from fear and anxiety
For He desires to meet our needs
Seeking first His kingdom and His righteousness is the vital key
I Peter 5:7; Matthew 6:33

For God takes notice of what we say within ourselves
Things which we dare not speak publicly out loud
All the little dark secrets that we keep hidden from the
ears of others
Least they be discovered by the crowd

It puts us in the proper state of mind as we come into His presence
Understanding that He is the Almighty and Supreme being
And yet He is compassionate and full of mercy
And He longs to forgive us and redeem
Psalm 103:4; Ezekiel 18:23,32

We should not strive for public recognition
But live a life of true humility
God wants a deep, intimate personal relationship with
each one of us
That is His heart's desire for you and me
Isaiah 49:16

A relationship that is personal and not public
As Christian's this should be our hearts desire from within
When we come into His holy presence
We should seek to glorify and honor Him

We should not be seeking the praise of men
But seek to grow in God's knowledge and His grace
Thus, our acts of righteousness and our prayers of devotion
Should be done in the "secret place"
II Peter 3:18

Yes, there are times we should pray together
And there are those who do so pray with true sincerity
For regardless of where they pray
They pray with true humility
Matthew 18:20

But it is the "in secret" relationship we have with God
That will help us turn from all hypocrisy
So as not to win a reputation for piety with our fellowmen
Turning us away from pride so we can walk in true humility
Luke 18:9-14

We should have an attitude of submission
We should draw close to God with respect, a reverential fear
We should recognize that His name is "hallowed" and that He is
"in Heaven"
And that our heart-felt prayers He longs to hear
Matthew 6:9

The prayer of the Pharisees was not prayed for the love of prayer
But they prayed when it gave them the opportunity
To be admired and applauded by others
Their prayers were not done with sincerity and humility
Matthew 6:5, 9

Secret prayer is to be done in private
We have a greater freedom when we pray this way
And it helps us to avoid ostentation
So as not to put ourselves on public display

Do we not shut our door when we wish to be alone?
Or when we have some special undertaking to do during our workday
Jesus means that just as we do in our household and in our business life
We should do as we come to pray

Sometimes our experiences can leave us spiritual numb
Emotionally empty, barren and dry
Where our soul seems destitute and impoverished
Leaving us in a state where we are even unable to cry

When we experience times of darkness and discouragement
When we find it hard to pray
When our feeble prayers seem to just bounce off the ceiling
When we simple do not know what to say

It may well be we have an oversensitive conscience
At those times, the thought of prayer may seem to us a bit odd
When we experience an overwhelming sense of self-condemnation
Too shameful to come into the presence of a holy God

Look at 1st John chapter three
Verses nineteen through twenty-two
A condition and a promise
They are there for me and you

John knew that we have a tendency
Not to use the power of prayer
When we feel crippled and unable to get up spiritually
He knew that Satan wants to hold us down and keep us there

But our confidence before God is because of what we
have in Jesus
And it should take precedence
Over our feelings of self-condemnation
I hope this is getting through and making sense

Because God is greater than our hearts
And our oversensitive conscience can be quieted and diminished
When we recall what Jesus said while on the cross
When He spoke the words for believers "it is finished"

God knows what best ministers to His gracious designs
His Word teaches that for those who love Him all things work
for the good
Even Satan's onslaughts and the fiery trials we experience
But today this is so misunderstood
Romans 8:28

He ordains all things according to the counsel of His will
And that will may bring bereavement, sickness, and loss
But that counsel never errs or makes mistakes
Remember Jesus and the cross

When the bloody sweat stood on his face
And all fear and trembling of man in anguish were upon Him
Knowing His purpose and His Father's will
Was to cleanse us of our iniquity and sin

He did not dispute the decree of the Father
But bowed His head and cried
"Not my will, but yours be done"
Shortly before He went to the cross and was crucified
Luke 22:42

When you have real business on hand with Heaven
Earnestly seeking God's wisdom or pleading for His mercy
and His grace
When the concerns of another life and another world are
pressing you hard
Withdraw and then close the door once you have entered the
secret place

It is not that God is more present
Because God is wherever you are at the time
Whether that be in church or in the workplace
Or casually driving along in your car is perfectly fine

The difference lies in us
We all feel it the instant we shut the door
In that instant we are already new creatures
The moment our knees hit the floor

For those who are fragile or elderly
No longer able to bend the knee
You can still come into God's Holy presence
With a heart of true humility

We feel this is our proper and true and best place
We say, "This is the house of our God: This is the gate
To the entrance of our Heavenly Father's presence
The heart's treasured way to communicate"

And if we keep the door shut long enough
And give things time to work, they will
Very soon our Father and us will be the whole world to each other
As we learn to come into His presence quiet and still
Psalm 46:10

If you pursue that kind of relationship
If you lay out your life to be a person of prayer
You will make continual discoveries of practices and expedients
of secret devotion
And you will experience God's tenderness and care

For He will carry you up to heights of heavenly mindedness
That you once never thought possible
For He will give to the heart that is earnestly asking
So that His Spirit in you will overflow
Luke 11:13

Yes, the Lord's Prayer is a model prayer
One for us to emulate and follow
And as we learn to mirror and reflect its purpose for our lives
Our prayers will not be empty, vain or hollow
Isaiah 29:13

Satan wants us to feel guilty
He wants shame to be the motive for our prayer
He whispers his accusations in our inner ear
Saying that God is not compassionate, nor does He really care
Revelation 12:10

But there is nothing further from the truth
Do not let yourself be blinded by his lies
For Satan is the father of deception
We need to see beyond his falsehood and disguise
John 8:44

But all the blame cannot be placed on Satan
We each have a choice to make
We each have a personal responsibility
If with God, we really want to communicate

You may be asking, what about me personally
Well, after reflecting on this poem
I feel my prayer life has often been very shallow
When I have come before my Father's throne

Oh, there are times I go a little deeper
But I feel I have such a long way to go
So as not to treat God as a chum or pal or buddy
Yes, for me there is still much room to grow

To learn to come into His holy presence
With awe-inspiring respect
To understand His attributes as revealed to us through Scripture
Which I have a tendency at times to approach halfheartedly
or neglect

Written for the glory of God

You see, this poem was inspired by other resources. But it is about a prayer life we should all aspire to. I know that it has been a challenge to me. I pray that it will also challenge you

Matthew 6:6. But when you pray, go into your room and close the door and pray to your Father who is unseen. Then your Father, who sees what is done in secret, will reward you.

7. The Privileged Planet

The search for purpose and for meaning
The search to unlock life's mysteries
Of the earth's significance in the universe
In our search can we unearth the hidden keys?

The search for earth's significance in our universe
Is it not just a search for worth?
Is our planet a lonely speck in the great enveloping cosmic dark?
In the vastness of the universe?

Philosophy and science have been challenged by this quest
For over two thousand years
Early perceptions were shaped by the work of the Greek scholars
Who had a following by those with inquisitive minds and listening ears

Aristotle and Tomolic taught that the earth set motionless in the heavens
That the earth was stationary
While the moon, sun and stars and other planets revolved around it
In their mind making the earth exceptional and extraordinary

This geocentric view was the foundation of western cosmology
For eighteen centuries
It took them that long to figure out
That they had been using the wrong keys

Then, in 1543 a Polish astronomer
Had a different key that would spark a revolution
His book "The Revolutions of the Heavenly Sphere's"
Would be the beginning of a dissolution

Nickolas Copernicus argued that the earth was not stationary
But instead orbited with the other planets around the sun
In the eyes of some this belief was to be that of a heretic
That God's earth was not the center of the universe or number one

But for the first time a correct understanding
Of the mechanics and structure of the solar system was in sight
Copernicus had a theoretical way of explaining these mechanics
Which were later proven to be right

The idea of a moving earth
Seemed to violate some foundational principle
But Copernicus somehow had the mental power
To imagine the impossible

And once you imagine the earth moving
That it was the earth traveling through space
That it and the other planets orbited the sun
The mathematics started falling into place

It all started making sense
The machinery of God's gigantic cosmic clock
It was the perfect golden key
That fit perfectly into the mysterious lock

Nickolas unlocked one of the great mysteries of the universe
He had laid the cornerstone for modern astronomy
Allowing for other doors to be unlocked as well
In the pursuit of scientific discovery

Yet 400 years after his discovery
There still seemed to be some deception and confusion
Instead of seeing intricacy and orderliness
Some embrace the theory of evolution

I think it would be wise to ask ourselves
Why do people do that?
Why do they believe fairy tales and embrace vain imaginations?
It is like believing in magicians who pull rabbits from a hat
II Corinthians 10:5

The empirical fact that our planet
Was not the center of our solar system has evolved
Into what is now known as the Copernican Principle
But embracing truth will quickly make that idea dissolve

The Copernican Principle is the idea
That our world occupies no preferred place in our universe
But that is not what Copernicus himself thought
For he knew the uniqueness and specialness of our earth

Copernicus had a theoretical way of explaining
The apparent motion of the planets across the sky
There was nothing mediocre about this man or about his theory
Do not even toy with such a lie

Nevertheless, this misrepresentation of the Copernican Principle
Became predominant in the 20th century
And in the realm of theories instead of science
It is often called the Principle of Mediocrity

You are the Salt of the Earth

This misrepresentation of the Copernican Principle
Says that our location is unexceptional
And that the earths status is mediocre
But that simply is not so

It says that we are in no way privileged
Or that our universe was not intelligently designed
That we as people should not assume that we are special
That our universe was not designed with beings like us in mind

This Copernicus Principle as well as the concept
Of the earth's insignificance was popularized
During the 1970's and 80's by the late astronomer Carl Sagan
Using propaganda and outright lies

The world on which we live
Is indeed a very special place
And God designed it to be inhabited
Inhabited by the human race
Isaiah 45:18

Written for the Glory of God

8. Heaven's Hope

What is your most valued possession as a person?
Ponder on this question and think it through
Is it not the precious life you have been given?
The gift of life that God has given you
Let Jesus become your most valued possession
Psalm 73:25-26

When we ponder on our earthly existence
We must face the reality
That our life will one day come to an end
That is true of you as well as me
Hebrews 9:27

Considering this fact, we have more questions
When we exit this life where do we go?
This is one of life's most important questions
For each one of us possesses an eternal soul
Matthew 25:31-46

The Bible is a book of revelation
What follows death does not need to be a mystery
For it answers life's most important questions
It is the Book that holds the key

Heaven is not a fantasy or a fairytale
It is not an imaginary place of make believe
God wants us to stay clear of Satan's playground
For Satan's purpose is to cause doubt and to deceive

Many churches have lost a sense of holiness
And what it means to grow in grace
What it means to sanctify ourselves as on to the Lord
Or what it means to earnestly seek His face
II Peter 3:18; II Corinthians 6:14-17; Joshua 3:5; Psalm 27:8

Our Heavenly Father wants our faith to blossom
He wants us to grow both in truth and love
To spend time in prayer and in His Word
And to set our hearts and minds on things above
Colossians 3:1

Jesus said He is preparing a place for us in Heaven
Where we as believers will spend eternity
A glorious, wonderful place in Heaven
And that is where we should long to be
John 14:3; Revelation 21:4; Philippians 1:23

Many are plagued with uncertainties in this life
And many are wandering aimlessly with no goal
Living only for the pleasures of this life
With no concern for their eternal soul
Matthew 14:31; Psalm 14:1; Luke 12:19

Peter asked this most important question
To where can a person go?
When Jesus asked if they too wanted to depart from him
For Jesus is the only one who can save a person's soul
John 6:68; John 6:67; Acts 4:12

Poems Of Inspiration

When we grasp the truth about Heaven
It will help us in the way we think
It will stir our hearts and change our thoughts
Sadly, today in many churches Heaven is a missing link

Heaven is the most encouraging subject in the Bible
Heaven is the happiest location in the universe
Scripture admonishes us to set our hearts and minds on things above
While we are still alive and walking on this earth
Colossians 3:1; II Corinthians 6:2

As Christians we should be anticipating Heaven
We should be looking foreword to that day
Pause, and take the time to open your Bible
And listen to what Peter had to say
II Peter 3:11-14

While living in this sin-cursed world
Satan wants despair and doubt to cloud our eyes
He wants us to feel helpless and hopeless
But the truth of Heaven will help us overcome his devious lies
John 8:44

The neglect of teaching on Heaven in our churches
Has caused us to grow indulgent, self-centered and weak
And neglect of other important doctrines in the Bible
Has caused us to lose the desire to ask and knock and seek
Matthew 7:7

Our concern about personal holiness has begun to slip away
And we are losing our passion to win lost souls to Christ
We are becoming spiritually lazy and indifferent
And as a result, we are losing the true purpose of our life
Proverbs 11:30

Many no longer have a spiritual hunger or thirst
Becoming comfortable with what this world has to offer
And as a result, the lost continue to remain lost
And we as Christians have no fear of being mocked at by the scoffer
Matthew 5:6

Our salt becomes worthless, and our light grows dim
And subtly we start to embrace this world's philosophy
We lose our appetite for the things of God
We have eyes but can no longer see
Matthew 5:13-14; Mark 8:18

So many have drifted from our first love
We no longer ask and knock and seek
Tearing at the very heart of our Heavenly Father
As a result, the church is frail and weak
Revelation 2:1-7; Matthew 7:7; Ephesians 4:30; 1st Thessalonians 5:19

Our Heavenly Father is not detached from His Creation
God has emotions and feelings too
And Jesus wept over hardhearted Jerusalem
And He died for me and you
Genesis 6:6; Luke 19:41-44

Heaven is a prominent theme in Scripture
Mentioned over 500 times in God's Word
In addition, the Bible presents a galaxy of related terms
It is a prominent theme but one that is seldom if ever heard

Did you know there is a plurality of Heavens?
In the Bible Heaven plays such a prominent role
But there is a silence and neglect on this topic within our churches
That such a place exists many sitting in the pews simply would not know

Poems Of Inspiration

The first Heaven is the atmospheric heaven
This first Heaven should bring a smile to your face
It is unlike any known atmosphere in the universe
This earth on which we live is a very special place

We live on a very privileged planet
Listen to what God's word said nearly 3000 years ago
Unlike the other planets He made ours to be inhabited
Where living things were made to blossom and grow
Isaiah 45:18

The psalmist referred to the second heaven
When he wrote, "The heavens declare the glory of God"
Evolutionary theories begin creation without a Creator
Their vain imaginations take them to a realm that is beyond just being odd
Psalm 19; II Corinthians 10:5

The second heaven is the vast universe in which we live
Filled with billions of stars and galaxies
There are more stars than grains of sand
The sands that line all the shores of all our seas

The story of the creation of the second Heaven
Is told in Genesis chapter one
"Let there be lights in the firmament of the heavens"
That is when God set in place the sun

And then we read of the third Heaven
Where the LORD has established His holy throne
This is where Jesus is preparing a place for Christians
It is our final dwelling place and our eternal home

The Apostle Paul got a glimpse of the third Heaven
He was caught up in that most glorious place
The experience was such a source of encouragement
To help him persevere and be steadfast in the race

The Third Heaven is the very dwelling place of God
And His kingdom rules over all
When we cannot even grasp the size of the universe
How can our view of Heaven be so small?
Psalms 103:19

Jesus mentioned Heaven about seventy times
In the Gospel of Matthew alone
How can those behind our pulpits be so silent?
On Heaven our eternal home

And what about the rest of us
Do we not have a responsibility?
Should we not be feeding daily on God's Word?
His love letter from Heaven to you and me

Most are familiar with the famous painting
Depicting Jesus on the night before His death
Sitting with His disciples in the Upper Room
Describing the details of how He would breathe his final breath
John Chapters 14-17

His disciples were confused and filled with sorrow
His words were illogical throwing their thoughts into confusion
I believe all sense of stability was lost
His words of death were a dark intrusion

But Jesus also spoke of Heaven
But I believe because of all their anxiety it created confusion
Allowing Satan to take advantage of their fear
So that at the time Heaven seemed to them no more than
a delusion

When death steals away someone we love
It causes one's thoughts to become incongruous and surreal
Such news can have a traumatic effect on its hearers
And have an adverse effect on the way they think and feel

Speaking of His betrayal and His imminent death
I do not think His disciples were prepared to hear such
shocking news
One's thoughts can become distracted and chaotic
Leaving one bewildered and confused.

But regardless of what they were thinking at the time
Jesus spoke the truth with clarity
Jesus spoke of preparing a real place in a real location
A "place" where Christians will spend and enjoy eternity

Sometimes Heaven is referred to as a country
A country implies a vastness of territory
Sometimes it is referred to as the Celestial City
Surpassing all cities with its splendor and its glory

When we think of cities, we think of buildings
We think of busy streets and activity
Billy Graham wrote "Heaven is God's habitation"
And Jesus is preparing a place there for me

Jesus spoke of Heaven in a personal intimate way
It is not an empty unoccupied vacant space
And we too like Jesus can call it "our Father's house"
Where Jesus is preparing for us a place
Matthew 6:6

I personally did not grow up in a loving home
A home filled with laughter, love and fun
My older siblings and I were taken from my father when I was
four years old
My mother had died when I was only one

Death, divorce and abandonment permeate our fallen world
Maybe you yourself never experienced a loving home
But regardless of what circumstances you are experiencing
The God of Heaven wants to claim you as His own

God does not want us to be religious
He wants an intimate relationship with me and you
He wants to be the Father of the fatherless
He wants to heal your brokenness so that you start anew
Psalm 68:5

Heaven is not just a benevolent state of mind
Nor is it a pie in the sky fantasy
It is not some sort of mystical utopia
It is where Jesus is preparing a place for me

It is just as real as the earth beneath our feet
And one thing the Bible makes very clear
As to its location Heaven is up!
And it will have an unadulterated heavenly atmosphere

Written for the Glory of God

Inspired by the book "Revealing the Mysteries of Heaven" by Dr. David Jeremiah. Please take the time to look up the Scriptures referenced in this poem and you may consider buying Dr David Jeremiah's book!

9. Hell, there really is such a Place

You would almost think there was no Hell
If you do not take the time to open up God's Word
Or if you sit in one of the many churches in our culture
For the word Hell is seldom if ever heard

Skeptics ask. "How can you say that God is a loving God?"
And at the same time believe in an eternal Hell?
They say such a doctrine is heartless and immoral
They say such a cruel doctrine we should dispel

Many unbelievers deny Hell's existence
As Christians we need to beware of the deceivers
For a little yeast works through the whole batch of dough
Causing doubt even amongst believers
Galatians 5:9

Is Jesus inhumane, cruel and barbarous?
When he warns humankind of eternal punishment?
Today, are Jesus' parables devalued as being worthless?
Considered by many to be in error, a mistake or a misprint

Was Jesus in error when He spoke of Hell?
Some ask, "What was Jesus thinking of?"
Surely, he was misrepresenting the God of Heaven
A God full of compassion, grace and love
John 14:9; Matthew 10:40; Psalm 145:8

In this pluralistic age it seems too harsh a punishment
Sadly, even Christians question the justice of Hell
They find the doctrine to be distasteful and repulsive
Something repugnant that we need to repel

Whatever else that may be said against it
The Christian doctrine of Hell cannot be an illusion
We need to examine the Scriptures about this horrid place
We need to study so we can clear up the confusion

The Gospels reveal to us the compassionate and humble Jesus
And no compassionate person wishes anyone to spend an eternity in Hell
That is why Jesus died on the cross for our sins
After repeatedly ringing the warning bell
Matthew 11:29; 1st Peter 3:18

If someone tortures and kills someone you love
Compassion is not the first feeling that we feel
Most likely we feel intense anger, hatred and a desire for revenge
I think it is time that we get real

How many times these words have flowed so easily
And Jesus said our words reflect our heart
The words, "I hope you rot in Hell"
Where do such seeds of hatred get there start?
Luke 6:45

Poems Of Inspiration

It is time we take the Scriptures seriously
And grasp the consequences of original sin
And the words spoken in the book of Revelation concerning Heaven
That nothing impure will ever enter in
Revelation 21:27

Jesus frequently taught on the existence of Hell
He took the topic of Hell very seriously
He gave a very graphic and vivid account of Hell in Luke chapter 16
And his parables are there for all to see

Nearly half of Jesus' parables
Warn of this dreadful place
It boggles my mind that any would choose to go there
And reject God's offer of forgiveness and His grace

All mankind was made in the image of God
And Jesus, being in very nature God clothed himself in humanity
He willingly descended from his rightful throne
And He willingly chose to die for you and me
Genesis 1:27; Philippians 2:6-11

There is something seriously wrong in our churches today
Those churches remaining silent on the topic of Hell
On those remaining silent on God's justice and His judgment
When God's love is the only story that they have to tell

It is not only Jesus that addresses this topic
Other inspired Scriptures address it as well
Perhaps the most vivid of all is found in the book of Revelation
Read chapter 20 and the dreadful story it has to tell

The Apostle Paul spoke of everlasting separation from God
And his words still ring true today
Of those who would be punished with everlasting destruction
Of those who close their ears and turn the other way
II Thessalonians 1:9; Matthew 13:15, 14:17-24

Jesus wept bitterly over Jerusalem
Over those who were unwilling to repent
Of those who sinned against the remedy
Rejecting the Messiah who had been sent
Luke 19:41; John 1:11

That they would be shut out from His presence
And from the majesty of his power
Today is the church ready for his appearing?
As we approach that final hour
Acts 1:11

"Man is destined to die once"
The writer of Hebrews added this note of finality
"And after that to face the judgment"
And after that there is eternity
Hebrews 9:27

God's love demands a Hell
Regardless of what men may say
Those that say the doctrine of Hell is eminently unloving
Yet the Scriptures clearly teach a Judgment Day

The Bible asserts that "God is love"
And love cannot act coercively
A God of love cannot force people to love Him
The Passion of Christ speaks persuasively
1st John 4:16

Poems Of Inspiration

A loving being gives space to others
He does not force himself on them against their will
One can reject the gift of a beautiful vase of flowers
Or receive it and place it prominently on a windowsill

God has set eternity in the hearts of men
But He allows mankind the freedom of choice
For Him to merely override a human will would be for Him useless
He desires to woo you with His gentle voice
Ecclesiastes 3:11; Genesis 2:16-17; Joshua 24:15; Revelation 3:20

Therefore, those who do not wish to love God
Must be allowed not to love Him if they choose
Such a choice will shut them out from the Lord's presence
For one to choose Hell is to eternally lose

For those who "do not" wish to be with Him
He must allow them to be separate from Him as well
And though He desires all to be with Him in Heaven
Many choose the broad road and wide gate that leads to Hell
Matthew 7:13-14

Human dignity demands a Hell
There is no denying that we exist
Well, there are some who deny this reality
And there are others who say God is no more than a silly myth

Those who claim to believe in such foolish nonsense
Those who say that we do not possess a soul
What is the reasoning behind such a belief?
What is their purpose and their goal?

They then put themselves in place of God
So that they can do just as they please
They will have no God ruling over them
I pray that you are not one of these
Judges 21:25

In the end there are two kinds of people
First, those who say to God, 'Thy will be done'
And the second kind is those who reject Heaven's invitation
To whom God says, in the end, 'Thy will be done'
C.S. Lewis

Forcing people to do something against their will
Is an affront to their dignity
God will respect one's decision to dismiss and to reject Him
Those who place themselves above His grandeur and majesty
Isaiah 14:12-17

Such people cannot deny that they have this freedom
The power to think and to believe
To pick up a Bible and examine the evidence
There is no reason for any to be deceived
Joshua 24:15; Galatians 6:7-8

The world we live in is filled with oppression and injustice
We are aware of all the discrimination and inequality
God's will is yet to be done on earth as it is in Heaven
Injustice takes place in every society
Matthew 6:10; Proverbs 31:8-9

It is a fact that we live in a sinful fallen world
And that people have the freedom to sin
And that they can choose to be selfish and reject God's standards
That they can choose to live independently of Him
Genesis 6:5; Joshua 24:15

As a result, cause and effect comes into play
The principle of sowing and reaping
The harvest will not be harvested unto the Day of Judgment
Until then we experience seasons of laughter and seasons
of weeping
Galatians 6:7-9; 1st Corinthians 4:5; Ecclesiastes 3:4

Laws and rules are necessary in a fallen world
In order to sustain stability
We need those with character, backbone and courage
To do the right thing in the face of adversity
Psalm 19:7-14

We are painfully aware that all evil is not punished in this life
That the wicked prosper in this life is plain to see
Thus, a place of punishment is necessary after this life
After this life we will all enter eternity
Psalm 73 read the whole chapter

It is not only the vilest who will enter through the gates of Hell
For the Word of God makes it very clear
That "all have sinned and fall short of the glory of God"
All one need do is investigate God's Word as if it were a mirror
Romans 3:23

We live in a country that murders its children
The most defenseless victims and the most innocent
Much of America's conscience has been seared as with
a hot iron
The world we live in is becoming more and more decadent
1st Timothy 4:2

God's sovereignty demands a Hell
Otherwise, God is not in ultimate control
There must be an ultimate separation of good and evil
And we all have an eternal soul

In society, punishment for evil is necessary
In order that good might prevail
It is Christ's death on behalf of those who believe
That gives the ultimate victory over death and Hell

The cross of Christ implies Hell
At the center of Christianity is the cross
For without it there is no salvation
Without it we all would be eternally lost
1st Corinthians 1:17-18, 15:3; Romans 4:25; Hebrews 10:14

It is the very purpose for which Jesus came into this world
The cross is the only way we can be delivered from our sins
We have a responsibility to take up the Word of God
Because so many false religions are being carried on the winds
Mark 10:45

We must ask, but why the cross unless there is a Hell
And why did the Father send His Son?
The cross is a sham if there is no Hell
The cross serves no purpose if there is no Hell to shun

Christ's death is robbed of its significance
Unless there is an eternal separation from God
From which sinful people need to be delivered
Please do not trample God's grace into the sod
Hebrews 10:29

Unbeliever's objections must be addressed
In face of Hell's reality
It is not difficult to understand why they wish there would
be no Hell
With its misery and finality

Some ask, "Why punish people? Why not reform them?
The answer is simple from both a biblical and rational point of view
It is the very heart of God to reform people
That is His desire for me and you

One should not delay in making this decision
The time of reformation is in this life
The Lord does not want any to perish but all to come to repentance
And to place their faith in Jesus Christ
2 Peter 3:9; II Corinthians 6:2

Unbelievers have everything to lose and nothing to gain
By not believing in eternal Hell
Read the story of the rich man and Lazarus
And the sad story it has to tell
Luke 16:19-31

The Lord is not slow in keeping His promise
He is patient with both me and you
The Lord does not want anyone to perish
With our freedom what will we choose to do?
II Peter 3:9; Joshua 25:14

However, after the time of reformation comes
The time of reckoning will come as well
And after man dies, they will face the judgment
And unbelievers will spend an eternity in Hell
Hebrews 9:27

Further, Hell is only for those who choose to be unreformed
For the reprobate and unrepentant
For those who choose to reject God's goodness and His love
For those who reject the One He sent
II Peter 2

God desires for all to be saved
God will not force free beings to be reformed
There is no room for any to be proud and arrogant
Spiritually that is why we need to be reborn
1st Timothy 2:4; John Chapter three

Men and woman are made in the image of God
They are not animals to be used or manipulated
Being made in God's image they are to be respected
Not exploited and abused and hated
Genesis 1:27

We have courts and judges and laws in this life
When crimes are committed against us, we want to see justice done
We see injustice and crimes each time we turn on the news
Quarrels about who should or should not own a gun

Some ask, is not eternal punishment overkill
They say in their heart that it is extreme
They bring accusations against the God of Heaven
Saying eternal punishment is cruel and mean

It does not matter how many excuses we entertain
So that we can continue in our sin
We make an eternal choice to receive or reject God's love
And one day we will give an account to Him

Well, why not have temporary punishment?
Why should there be any punishment at all?
We can try to reason and justify our sins
In order to have an excuse to reject the Saviors call

When we sin, we sin against the Eternal One
When we die physically, we will not cease to be
This may be wishful thinking for those who choose to sin
That their freedom will not require any accountability

Poems Of Inspiration

Some may honestly ask the question
If we know a loved one will be in Hell
How could we possibly be happy in Heaven?
Knowing where someone we love will ultimately dwell

What Christian has not struggled with this dilemma?
That is why we are persistent when we pray
That those we love would be receptive to the Gospel
And that from their sin their heart would turn away

Yet we cannot force our choice upon them
We must allow them to make their own choice
So, we pray earnestly and persistently
And pray that they will not tune out the Saviors voice

One's sin is an offence against a Holy God
And Heaven is a Holy place
Nothing impure or sinful will ever enter it
There will not be a hint of darkness not a trace
Revelation 21:27

Some ask, "Why did God create people in the first place?"
When He knew that some would choose to go to Hell
Again, they imply that God is responsible for the outcome
When in fact it is sinful people who choose to rebel

Some have said that life is like a game
If so, it is a very serious game we play
For there are rules and consequences in every game
If we decide to do things our own way

It is God's desire for all to be eternal winners in life
Not a selected few but everyone
For God so loved the "world"!
That He gave His Only Son
Ezekiel 18:23,32; John 3:16

Maybe a better analogy for life would be a marathon
A race in which everyone can win
It is an individual's choice whether to enter it
That will determine the outcome in the end

In the marathon of life, we run by faith
Crossing the finish line is our ultimate goal
It is our desire that those we love will join us
That they too would love the One who made their soul

It is sad to reflect on how many people
Give no thought to their eternal soul
How many live their lives indifferent to their Creator
Those who live life haphazardly with no eternal goal
Matthew 6:19-20

Most people do not have an eternal perspective
But for the Christian this should not be
They should have their hearts and minds set on things above
They should live their lives in light of eternity
Colossians 3:1-2

It does not matter if you are young or old
Death will one day steal your life away
The time to choose your eternal destination is now
Do not put it off another day
Proverbs 30:16; II Corinthians 6:2

The way we choose to live this life
Comes with great responsibility
Jesus' invitation to lost sinners is to follow Him
To follow Him and His standard of morality
Luke 12:48

God has given us the freedom to choose our destiny
Morality is not possible without freedom of choice
But our choices are followed by consequences
I plead with you to listen to His voice
Isaiah 1:18; Revelation 3:20

Jesus passionately desires all to be part of His Fold
But mournfully declares of some
"But you were not willing"
It is to those to whom God will say, "Thy will be done"
Matthew 23:37

Jesus and the Bible clearly establishes there is such a place
But let us look at the nature and location of Hell?
The Bible describes Hell in many forceful figures of speech
Let us listen what the Scriptures have to tell

Hell is described as a place under the earth
As a place "outside" the gate of Heavens city
It is described as a place of "outer darkness"
All of Hell's descriptions are far from being pretty
Philippians 2:10; Revelation 22:15; Matthew 8:12, 22:13

Hell is away from the "presence of the Lord"
The nature of Hell is a horrifying reality
In short, Hell is the other side of Heaven
It is not where one should desire to be
Matthew 25:41, II Thessalonians 1:7-9

It is like being left outside in the dark forever
Those who reject God will face a rude awakening
And one day everyone will bow their knee before the Lord
And every tongue will confess to Jesus Christ as king
Matthew 8:12; Philippians 2:11

The rebellious will bow down before Him as Lord and Judge
Before they enter through Hell's gate
I plead with you do not reject Heaven's invitation
You still have time its not too late

Hell is like a waterless cloud out in the desert
In a parched and weary land
Please listen to the gentle voice of Jesus
Reach out and take the Savior's hand
II Peter 2:17; Revelation 3:20

Hell is described as a perpetually burning dump
And as a bottomless pit
There is no prayer that will reverse this
Once one has entered, he will not get out of it
Mark 9:44-48; Revelation 20:1, 3

Hell is an eternal place
And no one can pray you out
And no one else can pay indulgences on your behalf
No matter how loud you scream and shout

Hell is described as an everlasting prison
There is no annihilation of the soul
One day our bodies will be resurrected
They will not remain in the grave or Sheol
1st Peter 3:19; John 5:28

Grave...Lake of Fire...
Underworld...Netherworld...Otherworld...Hades
Tartarus- *(Greek mythology)*
Sheol- *(Hebrew)*
Gehenna- *(Hebrew)*
Abaddon- *(Greek equivalent of Aladdin)*
Naraka- *(Hindi/Indian mythology)*
Inferno- (*From Dante's Divine Comedy)*

Luke says it is a place of anguish and regret
Hell is depicted as a place of eternal fire
The silence of the church on this doctrine is baffling
Many churches are in need of a "Town Crier"
Luke 16:28

A Town Crier shouts out the words "Hear ye, hear ye, hear ye"
This is a call for silence and attention
One day we all will stand before God's Judgment Seat
Death awaits us all there is no exception

This week you will make many choices
We all make choices all the time
We can choose to focus on the positive
Or we can choose to grumble and to whine

One can choose to do things his own way
And say to God, "Not your will but mine be done"
One can choose to reject the teachings of Jesus
And turn their back on both the Father and the Son

I will finish with this biblical principle
The principle of cause and effect
If you properly attend your garden it will be fruitful
Or it will become filled with weeds and almost fruitless because of neglect
I Corinthians 3:10-15

The freedoms we enjoy come with responsibilities
And if these responsibilities are neglected
Consequences will follow our abandonment
Consequences for our choices must be expected

Please put on your thinking cap
Do not live your life haphazardly
Do not live in denial and defiance
Make your choices in light of eternity

Written for the glory of God

Poem inspired from an article by Dr. Norman Geisler.
...a plea for sinners to be reconciled to God (II Corinthians 5:21) for their own sake and eternal well being.

10. Quest for character

God is an infallible Judge of every man's character
He knows of us what others can not see
He knows the secrets and hidden thoughts of every heart
Of course, that would include both you and me

This poem is about our character
And if we desire to do our best
Then it is our responsibility
To join with others on their spiritual quest

A mirror reflects our outward appearance
The Bible reveals what is hidden deep within
And for those who claim to follow Jesus
Our desire should be to be more like him

Spiritually, where are you today?
Compared to a year ago?
Where will you be a year from now?
Will you mature and grow?
1st Peter 2:2-3

Do you have a lifelong dream?
If so, are you pursuing it?
Or have you lost the vision of your soul?
Tempted to simply give up and quit
James 4:13-17; Matthew 6:33; Proverbs 29:18; Galatians 6:9

May I please ask a couple questions?
If you have a dream, is it God honoring?
Is it your desire to bring the God of Heaven glory?
Is your life a Christlike offering?
Romans 12:1

All hard work brings a profit
Do we not reap just what we sow?
But mere talk leads to poverty
If we do not plant the seeds, they will not grow
Proverbs 14:23; Galatians 6:7; Proverbs 14:23; John 12:24-26

What should we as Christian's be pursuing?
Is this not a question we should ask ourselves?
Are we spending time at the feet of Jesus?
Or do our Bibles sit unused on dusty shelves?
Philippians 4:8; II Corinthians 13:5; Philippians 2:12; Luke 10:38-42

One of the things a Christian should be pursuing
One of them should clearly be
Is to grow in Christlike character
That is true of you as well as me
II Peter 1:5-8

What is the definition of quest?
Words themselves are rich and meaningful
Some words are like sweet nectar to a needful heart
Such as grace and mercy to a sinful soul

Poems Of Inspiration

A quest is a pursuit, it is an adventure
It is a crusade, an exploration
It is inquiring and seeking while on a voyage
It is a journey and an expedition
Matthew 7:7

Before we begin our quest for character
Before we step up to the line to start
There is some cautionary advice found in the Scripture
We are forewarned to guard our heart
Proverbs 4:23

Webster adds a colorful dimension
To the definition of the word "quest"
It is "an adventurous journey pursuing a chivalrous enterprise in medieval romance"
In one's pursuit should not they give their very best
Matthew 22:36-40

Are you drifting downstream gathering debris?
Are you just floating effortlessly in the dross?
Is it your desire to live a life of ease?
Take no responsibility to carry your own cross?
Proverbs 25:4; Luke 9:23

Woven through the fabric of the New Testament
We see that God is forever on a quest
To transform us into the image of His Son
Should we not give Him our very best?
Romans 8:29; Philippians 1:6; II Timothy 2:15

As Christians, we are called God's "workmanship"
We are like clay in the potter's hand
And yet we are clay with responsibilities
This truth we need to grasp and understand
Ephesians 2:10; Isaiah 64:8; Romans 13:14

Character qualities in His children
This is our Heavenly Father's relentless quest
At times He will put us through the refiner's fire
To purge out the impurities in order to bring forth the very best
Hebrews 12:11; Colossians 3:23

Should not His quest be our quest?
Should not His goal be our goal?
Should we not desire to feast at the Lord's Table?
To allow Him to feed our soul
Isaiah 55:1-2

Life is like a jungle filled with predators
All one need do is glimpse at fallen humanity
We clearly see the depravity of the human heart
We start to see ever increasing insanity

Balance is a beautiful word
But at times it seems unattainable
With our own flesh and Satan raging against us
With so many enemies waging war against our soul

That is why the quest for character requires
A shield of protection around our heart
If we are to survive the onslaught of the jungle's predators
And avoid the poison of the serpent's stinging darts
Matthew 22:37-39; Ephesians 6:16

The Bible calls the heart our inner person
This is where truth is to be stored
We cannot walk through life haphazardly
God's provision simply cannot be ignored
Mark 7:20-23; II Peter 1:3

At times, the enemy's tactics can be subtle
Camouflaged and well disguised
Attacking us when we are weak and most vulnerable
Often mixing truth in with his lies
II Corinthians 11:4, 14

The things of this world should be used in moderation
We are not to overindulge ourselves in them
Again, that wonderful word known as balance
Symmetry is the key then we can win
1st Corinthians 7:30; Ecclesiastes 7:16

Where does the secret of contentment lie?
It will not be found in tomorrow or yesterday
It is found in that special block your holding
It is found in the block of time you have today
Philippians 3:13-14; Matthew 7: 25-34

Yesterday's nightmares are just that
But today unlocks tomorrow's dreams
What we build today will lead us into tomorrow
Tomorrow will be the result of today's progress and means
Philippians 3:13-14; Psalm 90:17

Yes, we must work to earn a living
But we also need leisure time
We need rest and relaxation
To help us to rise above the daily grind

Each day we have is a building block
What should be included in one's day?
Adding a little nutrition in your diet would be good
And setting aside a little time for rest and play
Proverbs 17:22

A day is a twenty-four-hour segment of time
Never lived before and never to be repeated
What you do today is of utmost importance
Each day earnestly desires to be entreated

A week consists of seven days
And each week comes to an end
And God has blessed Christians with the Lord's Day
A day we should rest and honor Him
Acts 20:7; Mark 2:23-28; Matthew 12:1-8

The Lord's Day is indeed a day of worship
That should be the sincere desire of a Christian's heart
The Lord's Day is the foundation day of the week
It is the weeks beginning its very start

Our worship is what we offer up to God
A good way indeed to start the week
But the Lord's Day goes beyond our songs of worship
Jesus said we are to ask and knock and seek
Luke 11:9

Worship is not just a Sunday thing
And although Sunday worship is a vital part
We worship God throughout the week
Each day of the week we are to dedicate to him our heart
John 4:23

There should be strong Bible-teaching from the pulpit
Church should be a place where saints are challenged
and equipped
Sunday school should bring balance to the body
With a strong emphasis on application and discipleship
Ephesians 4:11

It should be a place where we can be honest
A place where we can share our joys and share our tears
Where we can hold hands and pray for one another
Where we can share our victories and our fears

Responsibility in our quest for character is for all of us
The side of the pew you are on simply doesn't matter
The Word of God is multifaceted
Not only love but truth should be served upon our platter

The Word of God is unlike anything else
It is penetrating and powerful
It is living and active and searchers the human heart
It is spiritual nutrition for the soul
Hebrews 4:12

Today we are in need of the Master's touch
Though painful it may be
His surgery inevitably is beneficial
Preparing our hearts for ministry
John Chapter 15; Hebrews 12:11

Ministry in the sense of service
We should consider others before ourselves
First and foremost, this should take place in the family
Men take your Bibles off the shelves
Ephesians 4:12

In our quest for character
Let us not despise the Lord's discipline
Let us not grow weary of His chastening
Or of the correction that comes from Him
Proverbs 3:11

For the call to obedience is followed by promise
How much happier and fruitful we will be
As obedient children of our Heavenly Father
By the life-giving fruit that will grow upon our tree

Written for the Glory of God

11. If only I could Speak

Today a miracle is taking place
My new and unique life is about to start
My life's journey involves a continuous process
Before long I will have a beating heart

It seems God's people no longer have a zeal for justice
They act as if to say "we knew it not"
They act as if God's Word is no longer "living and active"
They shrug their shoulders as if to say that they forgot
Proverbs 24:11-12; Hebrews 12:4

A present-day holocaust is taking place
Right before our very eyes
And for so long we have turned our heads the other way
Are we willing to hear "a word to the wise?"

We speak of the church as being a family
What does a family consist of?
It is a husband and a wife and children
With boundaries to protect those we love

As Christians we have the very Word of God
We should handle it with tender loving care
For we are called to love the Lord with all our heart
And approach Him with earnest prayer
Matthew 22:37; James 4:8

We should have a tender place in our hearts for children
And those in the womb are the most innocent
They are precious in the sight of the God of Heaven
Regardless of their death being sanctioned by the government
Matthew 19:14; Acts 5:29

God has a special affinity in His heart for children
Children are a blessing and a sign of His favor
And God has a love for fallen humanity
As demonstrated in the sacrificial love of our humble Savior
II Corinthians 8:9

As Christians, we should examine ourselves
In light of this present-day holocaust
How sober and conscientious are we as Christians?
Today integrity and sobriety are subtly being lost
II Corinthians 8:9; 1st Peter 5:8; 1st Timothy 4:2: Titus 1:15

There are those who think they can shake off the restraints of conscience
But one day they will stand before a Holy God
Those who indulge in their sinful behavior before Him
And beneath their feet trample His truth in the sod
Hebrews 10:29

God pleads with all to come to their senses
He is ready to cleanse your conscience of every sin
O that you will no longer walk in a life of darkness
And that all would set their hearts and minds on Him
Proverbs 1:20-33; Isaiah 1:18; Ephesians 5:8; Colossians 3:1

Poems Of Inspiration

Today the process has begun
I am now well on my way
I will be twice my size in just twelve hours
I will grow in leaps and bounds with each new day

Yes, I am growing in leaps and bounds
God already knows that I am going to be a boy
My mommy will not know until a little later
When she finds out her heart will overflow with joy
Jeremiah 1:5

At the very moment of my conception
A true miracle has taken place
Just like countless others on this day
Together we have joined the human race

My sex was determined at that very moment
Complete with my own DNA
And sometime in the future I will make decisions
Decide what role in life that I will play

My story is the same as yours
It started at the point of conception
That is true of every human being
That is true of all there is no exception

From the very beginning of my life
If allowed to continue my journey and proceed
All I need is time, nourishment, truth and love
These are all that is needed for me to succeed

All my features are already set
This took place at the very moment of my conception
If only I could speak
I would ask you to discern God's truth from this
world's deception

What a wonderful gift God has given mothers
A female is uniquely different than a man
But it takes both to start a new life
It is God's design, his purpose and his plan
Genesis 1:27, 28 Genesis 3:20

In fact, before a female can get pregnant
Two people have to have sex with one another
Only then can a child be conceived
And then the young woman becomes a mother
Genesis 1:28

And God makes it very clear
That sex is to be only between a woman and a man
And only within the boundaries of marriage
Or deadly consequences will spread across the land
Leviticus 18:22; Genesis 2:24

If only I could speak
If only I could be heard
There is so much that I would say
But I am unable to utter a single word

In reality I am helpless and defenseless
I cannot speak a single word on my own
But there is a God who sees and knows me
My defense comes down from Heaven's throne
Proverbs 31:8-9; Proverbs 24:11-12; Jeremiah 1:5; Psalm 68:5

In just 4 weeks of my life's journey
There is a fact you may not realize
I have been growing very rapidly
I have already grown 10,000 times my original size

When I am just seven weeks of age
Every second 100,000 cells are being formed
And I will have two trillion cells
By the time that I am born

My mother is experiencing a sense of joy and wonder
For God has allowed her to share in life's mystery
And she and I will have a bond unlike any other
By the day of my delivery

The first sound that I will hear
Is the beating of my mother's heart
We have a significant relationship and attachment
Right from the very start

My mother's face will be the first face
That my infant eyes will see
The first caress that I will experience
Will be my mother caressing me

Yes, today a miracle is taking place
Inside my mothers' womb
It should be a haven for we the innocent
Not a sepulcher or a tomb

I am not evolving in this holy place
It is the place that has been prepared for me
I am in the process of development
This truth is very plain to see

Open up the Word of God
Psalm 139 is my defense
And open up your heart and mind
It is just simple common sense

The problem is not with us the unborn children
But with the sinful heart of humanity
If sins were like drops of water from the beginning
It seems humanities sins would overflow a bottomless sea

It is God Himself who placed me here
Safe in my mother's womb
And He proclaims woe to those who shed innocent blood
Those who turn it into a graveyard and a tomb
Proverbs 6:17

There is no one more innocent than a child
There is no one more vulnerable and weak
Then those who cannot stand up for themselves
It is those who know the truth and have a voice who are to speak

Though I am hidden from the outside world
I am not hidden from God's All-Seeing Eye
And the church has a responsibility
To expose the devil's lie
Ephesians 5:8

Miracle upon miracle is taking place
Today I just turned 17 days old
My blood vessels are starting to form inside me
My life's journey is worth being told

I am precious in the eyes of my Creator
A person of great value and great worth
It is He who determines personhood and gives life to all
And He longs to celebrate my birth
Matthew 18:1-5; 19:14

If I could speak, maybe, you would listen
Maybe you would see with spiritual eyes
Maybe the veil of deception would be lifted
Maybe you could see through all the devil's lies
  Matthew 13:15

Science has confirmed it
Conception is life's starting place
And the new birth Jesus spoke of
Starts with repentance and God's mercy and His grace

We live in a dark and fallen world
The killing of children is far beyond just being odd
This evil has been unleashed by the evil one
Instigated by the enemy of God
  Psalm 82:3-4; John 8:44

God's awesome power is displayed in His creation
And in procreation he has placed us in a very special room
The incarnate Immanuel God is with us
Jesus Christ shared in our humanity in a mother's womb
  Psalm 19; Isaiah 7:14; Matthew 1:23

This is one of the great mysteries of Heaven
Of the many this is only one
The love of a Father is displayed for fallen humanity
In the sacrifice of Jesus Christ his Son
  1st Peter 3:18

What is your most precious possession?
Is it not life itself?
Who was it that gave you this special gift?
For the answer take your Bible off the shelf
  Genesis 2:7

Since you yourself have not been denied this gift
How can you deny it of the child inside of you?
This child that is in your womb
This boy or girl is not an it but he or she is a who

On day 21 my heart is beginning to beat
Just one of the many milestones along the way
And as I continue my life's journey
My heart will grow stronger day by day

No veil can hide us from God's All-Seeing Eye
It is He who formed us in the secret place
Should we not humbly bow our hearts before Him?
For one day we will stand before Him face to face
Proverbs 15:3; Psalm 139:15; 1st Corinthians 13:12

At the very moment of conception
A new and unique individual is formed
Hollywood does not have anything on God's creative genius
When they say a star is born

The greatest gift God offers sinful humanity
Is the gift of eternal life
He offers grace, mercy and forgiveness
All are found in the person of Jesus Christ
Titus 2:11-12; Acts 4:12

Many churches are filled with "good people"
At least they are "good" in the eyes of man
But God has a standard for holiness and perfection
That so many do not understand
Isaiah 64:6

In this world mankind is born with a sin nature
Therefore, Jesus said we must be born again
Salvation is found in no other name
He is the only One who can cleanse us of our sin
Romans 3:23; John 3:3 Acts 4:12; 1st John 1:7

Are your ears opened to hear the truth?
Are you listening with your heart?
If you are truly seeking for God's understanding
Then an opened Bible is where you need to start
Mark 12:30; Proverbs 3:5-6; Jeremiah 29:13

Human sexuality is the instrument of our physical being
The gift of sex when opened with a heart of love
Not only brings pleasure but new life
And brings honor to the Father up above
Songs Of Solomon

Sex, sex, sex, sex, sex!
God celebrates sexual love!
Within the boundaries of marriage, it is special
This gift from Heaven up above

But God's boundaries have been broken
By the sinful heart of humanity
And it continues in a downward spiral
By those who embrace a lifestyle of depravity

I myself once embraced a sinful lifestyle
And at times sin still tugs at my heart
The new birth is exactly what it implies
From there the sanctification process will start

You are the Salt of the Earth

I lived my life for sinful pleasures
I broke the boundaries that God had set in place
But God is merciful and patient
And He extends to all His gift of grace

I am no longer building my house on sinking sand
Jesus said we are to build our house upon the rock
I am no longer indifferent to His Word
I take the time to ask and seek and knock
Matthew 7:7, 24, 26 Colossians 3:16

If only I could speak
If I could step outside of the womb
I would speak in all the schools across America
I would speak in each and every room

I would speak in the universities throughout the land
The supposedly schools of higher learning
And in all the churches to awaken their consciences
That the hearts of all would be discerning
1st Corinthians 3:18-20; 1st Timothy 4:2

Have you experienced the abuse of the evil one?
Has your heart become hard and cold?
You feel worthless, and that life is meaningless
Have you believed the lies you have been told?

Each person has a unique dignity and beauty
Though this is not true in the eyes of men
It is true in the eyes of our Creator
Though for some this is hard to comprehend
John 10:10

Have you ever felt like you were abandoned?
Left feeling insecure and on your own
Felt like you were deserted and cast aside
Feeling left outside in the cold and all alone

God Himself wants to be your Father
And Jesus wants you to be his friend
Though you may have been abused by this world's system
Like Jesus you can be glorified in the end
Isaiah 53

Because you are not an illegitimate child
You are not illegitimate in God's eyes
The Pharisees accused Jesus of being illegitimate
Such rubbish comes from the father of lies
John 8:44

If you are a child born of fornication
It is no fault of your own
Like in the days of Noah we live in a culture of fornication
Where many children are abandoned and left alone

But all that have God for their Father
And have a true love for Jesus Christ
Have become children of God by adoption
And receive the gift of eternal life

If than, one is not a child of God
Then there is only one alternative
They become as one of the crowds as in the days of Noah
A world under God's judgment that has gone adrift
John 3:19-21

You say such words are harsh and horrid
How can one make such a claim?
Because all are in need of Christ's redemption
Salvation is found in no other name
Acts 4:12

God created sex as a beautiful gift
But because He loves us, He set in place boundaries
To protect our heart as well as our bodies
To keep us free of heartache and disease

There awaits for you a brand-new story
But you are free, and you have to make the choice
Jesus said, "Here I am, I stand at the door and knock"
I plead with you to listen to his voice
Revelation 3:20

Listen to the hymn "Amazing Grace"
About this gift God offers me and you
God desires to sanctify your broken heart and life
And replace the old and make it new
Ephesians 2:8-9; II Corinthians 5:17

God's royal list of the righteous
Are written in His royal Book
Would I find your name penned in with His royal ink?
Would it appear there if I were to take a look?
Psalm 69:28

I am an unborn person a human being
Not just an observable statistic on a chart
At about 22 days of my life's journey
I will have a beating heart

I have been created in God's image
That means I possess personality
Self-transcendence and gregariousness and intelligence
A moral being with the gift of creativity

All these attributes will develop as I grow
And they will continue throughout my life
And I will grow in grace and knowledge
As I am being transformed into the image of Christ
Romans 12:2

I will have a need and desire for human companionship
I will grow in my capacity of knowledge and of reason
Especially as represented by the "male and female"
aspect of life
I will mature with each new passing season

I am now 9 weeks old in my mommy's womb
My fingernails and fingerprints are developing
I can now be seen sucking my thumb
And my nerves are functioning

My bones are beginning to harden
And my male organs now appear
I am now moving away from the wall of my mother's womb
But my mother's heart is very near

You see, our life starts at conception than continues
No matter what the stage
Infant, toddler, and preteen, adolescent
And no matter what our age

Teenager or young adult
As the years keep passing by
That life starts at conception and ends at death
Is a fact we cannot deny

God has made me "a little lower than the heavenly beings"
And He has crowned me with a crown of glory
My human dignity is derived from God Himself
Meaning, purpose and dignity are included in my life's story
Psalm 8

Being made in the image of God
I will follow His standard of morality
As I grow, I will be able to distinguish truth from lies
Enabling me to clearly see

If only I could speak
I could make choices just like you
I would speak up and defend myself
Like you yourself so often do

The eyes of the Lord are everywhere
What you do is not hidden from His sight
The slaughter of the innocent is a scourge upon our nation
This darkness has now been brought into the light
Proverbs 15:3; Luke 8:17; Ephesians 5:8-16

God does not want you to remain in your brokenness
He wants to bring healing to your soul
He wants you to receive His seed into your broken life
And to nurture it so it will grow
Matthew 11:28; John 1:12; 1st Peter 2:2-3

If only I could speak
That all would listen would be my prayer
That you would listen with your heart
That you would really care
Genesis 4:10-11; Hebrews 12:24

Today I can pucker up my brow and my eyes can squint
And I am only 10 weeks old
My voice box is forming, and I can swallow
Before your very eyes, my life story is being told

Poems Of Inspiration

It is obvious to a casual onlooker
Though I may be physically hidden from their eyes
That there is a new life taking place inside my mother
There is no excuse for anyone to believe the devils lies
Romans 1:20

If I could speak, I would speak with pictures
For the adage is quite true
That "A picture is worth a thousand words"
And ultrasounds are there for all to view

Science has been very instrumental
Of showing life within the womb
Enabling you to observe my life from my conception to my birth
Like a flower from a tiny seed till it is fully bloomed

Ultrasounds are a tool used for God's glory
Used as a window to the womb
Shattering all deception and duplicity
Allowing you to glimpse into this sacred room

When I am welcomed into this world
My sister Dakota will be surprised
When she looks at my little fingers
She will be filled with curiosity when she looks into my eyes

What other words would leave my lips?
What other words would I speak?
I would plead all would heed the words of Jesus
This One who said for us to ask and knock and seek
Matthew 7:7

Because we live in a pluralistic society
Our minds are flooded with so many different choices
Many of which are deceptive and exploitive
Tempting to allure our ears with their deceptive voices

At 12 weeks of my life's journey, I can swallow
And mom's nutrients are passed on to me
Just 2 hours after she eats a meal
That is because I am special, an important VIP

My brain is beginning to mature
A process that will continue many years
Full maturity does not happen on the day that I am born
Maturity does not just magically appear

We see the miraculous hand of God
In the process of life at all its different ages
Each moment and phase in its development
At each point of time at different stages

The Word of God speaks for children in the womb
And His proclamation is very clear
And Jesus said "Let the little children come to me"
Children are close to His heart and very dear
Matthew 19:4

How can the church be silent?
Sit idly by and not say a word
Close their ears to the Word of God
And act as if they had not heard

If God speaks so highly of me
Then it only seems to make common sense
That the followers of Jesus would speak up on my behalf
Christians should not be known for sitting on the fence

Life has a beginning and an end
Take the time to think it through
Your first nine months were your foundation
That is true of me as well as you
Ecclesiastes 3:1-11

On day 28 my two tiny arms are making their appearance
And my thyroid gland is beginning to grow
And my blood vessels are beginning to function
And my own blood is beginning to flow

If only I could speak, what would I speak of?
I would speak of this most holy place
Where I am being fearfully and wonderfully woven together
My toes my fingers and my face
Psalm 139:7

Some say that I am not a person
How little do they know!
Life from the beginning to the end is an ongoing process
A lifelong journey where we grow

Each side of my brain has a billion cells
And today I am only 20 weeks old
I am a very special and unique person inside of my mother
So, you can discard all the lies you have been told

We tell children children's stories
But young adults need to hear the truth
For there are many who want to take advantage of their vulnerability
Those who for selfish gain would abuse and exploit our youth

When Cain murdered his brother Abel
God said Abel's blood cried out from the earth
Imagine the cry of the unborn millions
Never getting a chance to experience their birth

The Bible says you shall not murder
Yet today you live in a society
Where human life is being devalued
Where many put more value in unborn animals than of me
Exodus 20:13

The cry of Abel's blood is very powerful
This blood that cries out from the ground
And it has reached the God of Heaven
It is not some minute insignificant sound

The killing of Abel was just the beginning
The violent act was just the start
The violence continues to this very day
Revealing the darkness of the human heart

From there the murder of the innocent would escalate
Sin and violence and the shedding of innocent blood
And it would bring God's judgment on a sinful world
By means of a worldwide flood
Genesis 6:11; Genesis 7:7-23

Killing and human violence
Is seen throughout recorded history
That there is evil in the heart of men and women
Is not some hidden mystery

At 6 months my sweat glands are developing
And I find my favorite position in which to sleep
It will not be long now that I will hear my mommy praying
Dear Lord, I pray his soul to keep

If I were to be born prematurely
At this age I could survive
Just another fact that proves the truth
That inside my mother's womb I am very much alive

*My lungs are fairly well developed now
And at times mom finds herself giggling
And I am often referred to as precious cargo
It will not be long before I hear my mommy sing*

There are those who kill the innocent
Acting as if their innocent cries to God cannot be heard
And there are those who do not speak out against this injustice
Those who remain silent and do not speak a single word
Proverbs 6:17; Proverbs 31:8

Though their screams may be silent to our human ears
God's voice cries out "What have you done?"
To those who would murder their own children
Those who would put to death their own daughter or own son

There are those who try to silent this voice of conviction
They think they can successfully nail it to a tree
And take no responsibility for their guilt
That for their transgression they will give no accountability

Do you honestly believe that our Creator?
Cannot see every evil deed we do
Though we might think we can sin in secret
Our sins are not hidden from God's view

But there is another cry of great importance
That went up to Heaven from the cross
"Father, forgive them" sounded from the wounds of Emmanuel
From the One who came to seek and save the lost
Luke 19:10

The blood of Abel was not voiceless
And the blood of Jesus is not mute
It speaks for us and not against us
His blood does not leave us destitute
Genesis 4:10; Hebrews 12:24

You are the Salt of the Earth

Jesus was the innocent lamb slain on the alter
Bleeding from its death wound
Afterward his body would be shrouded in the darkness
And would be placed inside an earthly womb
John 1:29

From the very day of his conception, He was sinless
To the very day of his death
The faithfulness of Jesus made complete are redemption
The day he took his final breath

If I could only speak
My words might bring to your eyes some tears
For I would speak of the murder of my brothers and my sisters
And the hideous ways they have died throughout the years

If you could see the disturbing graphic pictures
Maybe it would open up your eyes
And bring conviction to your conscience
For it would expose the cultural lies

If only I could speak, I would say thank you
To all those who are not afraid to speak
Those who understand true justice
Those who take a stand for us the helpless and the weak

If only I could speak
What is it I would speak of?
I would speak of Jesus death upon the cross
And his sacrificial love
John 10:18

If I could speak, I would tell you
How I am progressing along the way
How I am wonderfully be woven together
How much I am growing day by day
Psalm 139

If only I could speak
I would speak of your pursuit of happiness and liberty
But I will never utter a single word
If life and liberty itself is denied of me

By now it is no longer a great mystery
It has been revealed that I am a human being
Truth once hidden from your mind and eyes
Is no longer cloudy but clearly seen

Repent and I will bring healing to your land
For your sin has left behind a trail of shame
Come to the foot of the cross of Jesus
For salvation is found in no other name
Acts 4:12

Soon I will be making my grand appearance into the world
But I will still have a long way to go
As the adventure of my life-journey continues
I will need much love and encouragement as I grow

I wonder what my future holds
What plans God has for me
I can hardly wait for my arrival
I wonder what my name will be
Jeremiah 29:11

Someday I will have children of my own
And in the future grandchildren too
Because you made the right decision to bring me into this world
Mom it is all because of you

I have only shared a few of the miracles
Miracles that have been placed before your eyes
Knowing the truth of life inside of the womb
Leaves you without excuse to believe the devils lies

Written for the glory of God

12. The Grandeur of God

How much do we really know?
Of the God we claim to love
And honestly how deep is our desire
To set are minds and hearts on things above?
Colossians 3:1

How, for example, do we know God?
Is it by reason, by revelation?
Is it by faith, by proxy, by direct access?
Is it by deep reflective thought and contemplation?
John 8:55

What role does human freedom play?
In a universe where God is sovereign over all?
What is the origin of evil?
And can one really be free apart from obedience to God's law?
John 1:12; Romans 11:33-36; John 14:21

How does one distinguish right from wrong?
Is there any basis for meaning and morality?
Is there really such a thing as good or evil?
Does one particular worldview hold the key?

Today, so many people fail to wear their "thinking cap"
As a result, brainwashing has become an easy thing
So many in the church fail to seriously examine the Scriptures
That is why so many false religions have a following

It seems like so many in the church are spiritually naked
Failing to clothe themselves with Jesus Christ
The One who shed His precious blood for our cleansing
The One who said I am the way the truth the life
Isaiah 61:10; Romans 13:14; John 14:6

The Bible clearly teaches there is a false church
That there are false teachers who purposefully deceive
That is why sound doctrine is so important
We need to know what it is that we believe
Matthew 7:5; 1st Timothy 1:1-5

Self-examination is well overdue
It is time to dig deeper and to search
And ask ourselves some of the hard questions
For example, "What is the true meaning of the church?"

One's worldview plays a central and defining role
In how they live from day to day
A worldview is how we interpret our experiences
Our thoughts, our actions, even the games we play

Our worldview and the worldviews of those around us
Have a huge influence on our society
Producing fruit that permeates the culture in which we live
As a result of the roots beneath the tree
Psalm 1

That is why it is so important for the Christian
To be grounded in God's Word
So that they can distinguish truth from falsehood
Because for many, truths cannot be clearly seen or heard

Every one of us has a "thinking cap"
And as Christians, we you are to "love the Lord with our entire mind"
It is included in the "greatest commandment"
Our intellect should be liberated and unconfined
Mark 12:28-34

Many non-Christian worldviews abound
We live in a pluralistic society
Therefore, it is fitting that we get acquainted with a theistic worldview
That way we can discern the apostles of absurdity
Matthew 7:15; Proverbs 14:12

Each worldview considers the following basic issues
It considers the nature of the universe
The nature and character of God or ultimate reality
The origin of humanity and the earth
Genesis Chapter 1; John 1:1-3; Isaiah 6:3; Genesis 1:27

It considers the question of what happens to a person at death
It considers the basis of ethics and the meaning of history
It considers the basis of human knowing and understanding
All these should be of great interest to you and me
Hebrews 9:27

The Bible is a book of God's revelation
And it reveals a theistic worldview
It makes sense of our life, our world, our universe
It is God's gift to me and you
II Timothy 3:16-17; James 1:17

It reveals God as being infinite and personal
It reveals God as transcendent and immanent
A personal God involved in the world that He created
A personal God involved in people's lives as well as government
Acts 17:27; Romans Chapter 13

It reveals the omniscient God of Heaven
A sovereign God who is good
But because of the sinful nature of fallen humanity
He is a God who is often misunderstood

Many worldviews are filled with inconsistencies
And they crumble from within
And under true examination
They blow away with a howling wind

Deism views God as being impersonal
Referring to Him as a Force, or Energy, or First Cause
The only explanations that they can come up with
About as personal as Santa Claus

As something to get the universe running
They often capitalize it to give it an aura of divinity
But surely not a personal God who has revealed Himself
And showing His love to us on Calvary

To know Jesus is to know the Father
The One who came to show humanity its worth
Emmanuel, God is with us
He shared in our humanity when he walked upon this earth
John 14:9; Matthew 1:23

He came into this world to show us how to live
He came to show us how to love
He came to teach us by his example
That we should set our hearts and minds on things above
John 13:34; Colossians 3:1-2

We see that He was personal and intimate from the beginning
Where in the Garden He walked with Adam and Eve close by
their side
But after they sinned close fellowship was broken
In their nakedness and shame the two of them were
quick to hide
Genesis 3:8; Genesis 3:10

But God still came to the two of them in the Garden
It was not He who turned and walked away
It was not His desire to extinguish the intimacy
He came to them in the cool of the day

But instead of acknowledging and confessing their sin to God
The two of them were quick to cast the blame
Sin often tends to want to excuse itself
And by doing so added to their shame
Genesis 3:11-13

But even after their failure to acknowledge their wrongdoing
And their trying to cover their nakedness and shame
God Himself provided them with a covering
And we get a glimpse of why Jesus came

Because it took the shedding of innocent blood
Manmade coverings and efforts will never suffice
It is God Himself who would provide the Lamb
Jesus would place himself on the alter as the perfect sacrifice
John 1:29

Look, the Lamb of God!
This was John the Baptist' great proclamation
The means by which sinful man can be reconciled back to God
For it was the proclamation of emancipation
II Corinthians 5: 17-21

Yes, God is real, and He is personal
And He desires a personal relationship with you
Jesus is standing at the door of your heart with an invitation
The invitation goes out to all not just a few
Revelation 3:20

Please remove the fig leaves of your own making
Come before God with true humility
And receive the free gift of salvation that God has offered you
For we have all eaten fruit from the forbidden tree
Genesis 3:7; Psalm 51:17

Written for the glory of God

Matthew 4:4. But Jesus replied, "It is written: Man shall not live on bread alone, but by every word that proceedeth out of the mouth of God.

John 1:1-2. In the beginning was the Word, and the Word was with God, and the Word was God. He was with God in the beginning.

John 1:14. The Word became flesh and made His dwelling among us. We have seen His glory, the glory of the one and only Son, who came from the Father, full of grace and truth.

13. Satan's Goal

Satan is not a fictitious character colored red
Satan does not have horns, a pitchfork and a tail
He influences CEO's and presidents and rulers and pastors
Not just those whose crimes put them in jail

Today we live in a society of the walking dead
A culture that is embracing a death fantasy
Violent movies, and unrestrained sexual perversion
Multitudes sitting in a trance in front of their TV

Satan is manipulative and corrupt
He does indeed have a strategy and a goal
And he is persistent in his deadly pursuit
His desire is to steal away person's very soul

And he has attained his goal in the hearts of many
And although he cannot snatch a Christian from the Father's hand
He is always striving to make the Christian stumble
Dulling the Christian's conscience is part of his diabolical plan
John 10:28-30

He is always subtlety tempting us to eat the forbidden fruit
And he is often successful with the immature and the weak
That is why Christians are called to put on the full armor of God
That is why Jesus told us ask and knock and seek
Genesis 3:1-4; Ephesians 6:10-20; Matthew 7:7

He loves to see those in positions of authority
Stumble and fall into some hideous sin
He strives to keep the immature desensitized and vulnerable
Trying to convince them a victory they can never win
I Corinthians 10:12; I Peter 5:8

The conscience is the souls automatic warning system
That is why we as Christians have a great responsibility
To daily come into God's presence and feed on His Word
Feed on the rich delicacies He has provided for you and me
Matthew 6:11; Psalm 34:8

An educated, sensitive conscience is God's monitor
Meant to keep our heart under a systematic review
It alerts us to the moral quality of our lives
Of what we do or should not do

It warns of lawlessness and irresponsibility
It is meant to help us feel healthy guilt and shame
It is meant for us to take personal responsibility for our own actions
So as not to cast our guilt on others or to point the blame

Satan's strategy is sometimes slow and subtle
Successful at exchanging truth for lies
If he is unable to kill the Christian's conscience
Then his goal is to make it desensitized

Satan's task is made easier in a godless culture
And when the moral structure of the church starts to deteriorate
When it can no longer be distinguished from the surrounding culture
When it loses its salt and light it loses its God-given ability to communicate
Matthew 5:13-16

Are guilt feelings always erroneous and hurtful?
Or do the guilt feelings we feel serve a purpose?
We need to ask, what role does the conscience play in the life of a Christian
A non-Christian should ask what role does the conscience have to do with us?

Have you ever asked yourself, "What is the conscience?"
Today, many say it is a defect that robs people of their self-esteem
That it is a disorder that we need to get rid of
That it is an enemy that is cruel and mean

But far from being a defect or disorder
God designed it into the very framework of the human soul
Our ability to sense our own guilt is a tremendous gift from God
In the process of sanctification, it plays a vital role
John 17:14-19

The conscience serves as an automatic warning system
To guide us in the right direction and keep us alert
The conscience acts as a God-given compass
If followed will keep us from undo hurt

Human beings are made in the image of God
Our conscience is at the heart of what distinguishes us from
the animals
Animals do not contemplate their own actions and make
moral decisions
But God planted the conscience in human souls
Genesis 1:26

Animals do not build houses of worship
Animals do not feel guilt over sin
Animals do not live by reason but by instinct
They have no desire to worship God and honor Him

Animals do not form judgments by a process of logic
They have no need to justify their animalistic behavior
They have no need to offer up sacrifices to the living God
They have no need of a Redeemer or a Savior

No, being made in God's image people are not animals
But when people turn their back on Him
They can be worse than the cruelest animal
When they allow wickedness to dwell within
Jude 1:10

It is not the healthy who need a Doctor
And the sickness that all mankind has is sin
But the medicine prepared will not cure the patient if it
is not taken
And the Gospel is the only cure, the medicine
Luke 5:31; Romans 6:23

The light of nature and the light of law
Reveal the wrath of God from sin-to-sin
But many hold the truth as a captive like a prisoner
So that it should not have influence over them
Romans 1:18-32; Matthew 13:15

The heart that does not acknowledge its own unrighteousness
Is like a dark dungeon where its possessor threw away its precious key
A dungeon in which a many good truths are detained and buried
A heart that becomes a dungeon that refuses to set these captives free
Proverbs 30:20

Creation reveals the divine nature and power of the Creator
We know that things do not make themselves
God reveals Himself in nature and through the Scriptures
Yet so many Bibles sit unopened on dusty shelves
Romans 1:20; Psalm 19; Job Chapters 38-39

It is true that the Bible contains some things that are hard to understand
But the moral principles are very clear
And Jesus repeatedly made this statement
Those who have ears must let them hear
II Peter 3:16; Matthew 11:15

Mark Twain once made this statement
His conscience once being in tune with God's displeasure of sin
Said "it is not the things in the Bible that I don't understand that scare me
That frighten me and cause terror within"

At one time his conscience was pointing out his moral failure
His conscience was severing its God-given role
But for all that I have read and heard about him
He died hardhearted and with a bitter soul

It is the foolishness and practical wickedness of a sinful (sin full) heart
That clouds and darkens the intellectual powers and faculties
By those who embrace the foolish deceptive philosophy of evolution
My prayer is that you are not one of these
II Peter 2:17

One of those who professes to be wise
Not only is this dangerous but rather odd
For one to discard all the intricate designs we see in nature
And claim that did not come forth by the Hand of God
I Corinthians 3:18 Isaiah 40:26

Some say, "I cannot believe in a God I cannot see"
But nature and Scripture make it very clear
That the spiritual invisible things of God are clearly seen
Creation reveals God's divine power and nature as in a mirror
Romans 1:20

Things we cannot see with the naked eye
Air, our thoughts and electricity
An 8-month-old child in their mother's womb
And that great mystery known as gravity
Romans 1:20; Hebrews 11:1

We know x-rays and gamma rays exist
Or a dead skunk that is distant and out of view
And the pleasant aroma of grandma's homemade bread still in the oven
We know these exist through the senses God has given me and you
Proverbs 20:12

The Spirit of God is reflected in the hearts of Christians
Satan is reflected in the hearts of non-believers
Though at times Satan appears as an angel of light
As Christians we need to beware of the deceivers
Matthew 5:13-16; John 8:44; II Corinthians 11:14; Matthew 7:15

It is well for us that the Gospel
Reveals the justifying righteousness of God from faith-to-faith
For the Christian justification is followed by sanctification
As we grow in the knowledge of God's benevolent grace
Romans 1:17; II Peter 1:5-7; II Peter 3:18

Draw near to God and He will draw near to you
You will start to experience the invisible with spiritual eyes
Over time the invisible will become visible
You will start to distinguish God's truth from Satan's lies
James 4:8; Luke 10:24; I Corinthians 2:10; Matthew 13:11; I Peter 2:2

Slowly you will find the ordinary becoming extraordinary
If you are diligent in your search for truth
The designs and intricacies you will find in nature
Will flood you with overwhelming proof
Matthew 7:7; Romans 1:20

We know that gravity exists
And yet it remains a mystery
As well as our thinking process and our thoughts
That reside inside both you and me

The conscience is a distinct human innate ability
Enabling us to distinguish between wrong and right
It is there to perceive or point out a moral failure
It distinguishes between spiritual darkness and spiritual light
Ephesians 5:8

Poems Of Inspiration

The "good news" about salvation
Starts with the bad news about sin
Repentance is turning to the light of the Gospel
And acknowledging our darkness that lies within
Matthew 18:1-5; Luke 18:13

We see history repeating itself
When a people become hopelessly enthralled with their own sin
Nation after nation being abandoned by the God of Heaven
After they first abandoned Him
Judges 21:25

No one can plead ignorance to God's existence
They will be without excuse on Judgment Day
Are you one who is suppressing the truth in unrighteousness?
Turning your back on a Holy God while walking the other way?
Romans 1: 18, 20 Psalm14:1

Once a people begin to suppress the truth in unrighteousness
A spiritual darkness starts to spread across the land
Righteousness exalts a nation, but sin is a disgrace to any people
This truth we seem to fail to understand
Proverbs 14:34

One should ask, "Is there hope for those with a hard heart?"
The answer is yes, we see it again and again
The offer to repent and receive forgiveness is freely given to
the sinner
The hard-hearted need to return to God, turn to Him
Ezekiel 18:23, 32

What was once shocking and unacceptable behavior
Not too far in the distant past
Is now standard fare on network television
How long can a dark and decadent society last?

The devil has planted seeds in the hearts of many
Convincing people that he does not exist
And even multitudes who sit in our churches today
Think of him as no more than a silly myth

There can be no salvation for those who are not convinced
Of the seriousness of their sin
Those remaining oblivious to their estrangement from God
Those denying the sin-nature that dwells within

God is not cryptic or ambiguous
He and His truth are clearly seen
Today the church is once again in need of solid food
For there are many eating baby's food in need of being weaned
Hebrews 5:12; I Peter 2:2

How does this hardening of the conscience begin?
This downward spiral of depravity?
Leading to corrupt religion and uncontrolled lust
And sexual perversion, degradation and debauchery

Once people begin to suppress the truth in unrighteousness
Once they turn their back on the light
All that remains is spiritual darkness
People who choose to be dwellers of the night

The more we see the wonders of creation
The more we study the harmony of the universe
The more it reveals the order and wisdom of the One who designed it
The One who made this special place that we call earth

When people suppress the truth from their own consciences
Their minds start embracing vain imaginations
Thus, we see the civilized become uncivilized
Look at our own and other nations
II Timothy 4:3-4

Look at what happened to Sodom and Gomorra
Look at the world at the time of Noah's flood
Look at the time that history was divided
When mankind nailed Jesus to the cross and spilled His precious blood
Genesis Chapters 6-9

A world filled with animosity and hatred
As if two World Wars is not enough
To convince us of the fallen state of humanity
As well as the bent of sin that resides in each one of us
Romans 3:23

Even though there are built-in consequences for sinful behavior
People continue to raise their fist to Heaven and yell
We will not submit to your rules or beg your pardon
And ultimately their rebellion will lead them straight to Hell
Hebrews 9:27; Proverbs 19:3

Incurable diseases as a result of sexual perversion
Drug related deaths are on the rise
Misguided youth heading down the broad road of destruction
Influenced by a culture embracing Satan's lies
Romans 1: 27, 32; Matthew 7:13

With all the advancement in scientific knowledge
With their worldly wisdom, fools profess themselves to be wise
Rejecting truth, the death of common sense is soon to follow
Leading to a nation's downfall and demise
Romans 1:22

Refusing to honor God they lack spiritual understanding
Even their rational faculties are corrupted by their unbelief
Reaping the consequences of their rebellion
They still fail to repent and turn to God and cry out for relief
Revelation 6:16-17

Those who say in their heart, 'There is no God'
They are fools in the most profound sense of the word
For the evidence of God is overwhelming
Yet they remain willingly ignorant and undeterred
Proverbs 14:1; II Peter 3:5

Moral foolishness inevitably corrupts spirituality
And since mankind is inherently religious
Corrupt religion replaces true spirituality
A relationship with God is replaced with a religion that is insidious

Our public schools can no longer teach the Bible
Holiness and purity are becoming obsolete
And the same is true in many churches
Satan's goal is to make their downfall final and complete

Yet corrupt religion is flourishing throughout the world
The worship of self and idols is nothing new
Idolatry, witchcraft, hedonistic pursuit of pleasure
We choose in our heart what we desire to pursue

Corrupt religion exchanges the glory of the incorruptible God
Corrupt religion misrepresents and perverts the truth
Adults embracing a lifestyle of immorality
And encourage it in our youth

The first commandment is, "You shall no other gods before me"
Yet people tend to choose a deity of their own making
Remember Satan's proposal in the Garden
"Eat, it is there for you for the taking"
Exodus 20:2

Primitive paganism and the worship of Satan
Today is very much alive
Things unheard of in our nation 50 years ago
Have been awakened and revived
Matthew 4:19

In so many of our churches today across America
Biblical doctrines and moral standards are considered unrealistic
If you speak of holiness and repentance
You will fall under the accusation of being legalistic

Replacing God and the truth about Creation
Public schools teach our children that they are evolving
While the truth is just the opposite
As a result, they are morally de-volving

Instead of ascending into freedom and illumination
They are descending into a pit of dark depravity
In a downward spiral of sexual perversion
We are seeing this more and more in our society

Individuals and societies become self-destructive
And those who feed their lusts are judged accordingly
God gives them over in the sinful desires of their heart
To ever increasing debauchery and impurity
Romans 1:24

This speaks of the judicial act of God
Whereby He withdraws and withholds His restraining Hand
From an individual or a group in a society
This hardening is increasingly spreading across our land

In other words, God allows the principle of the harvest to take place
We do indeed reap just what we sow
God allows the consequences of sin to run their disastrous course
Once the yeast works through the batch of dough
Galatians 6:7

Is there hope for those traveling on this road of destruction?
Yes, for the God of Heaven has made a way
He has provided a Gate through which one must enter
In order to escape the wrath that is to come on Judgment Day
Matthew 7:13

The invitation to enter the Gate is open to all
But as we review and reflect on history
This invitation is only accepted by a small minority
To me this is a sad and bewildering mystery

But you are the one reading this poem
The decision to enter the Gate is up to you
Will you close the door of your heart to Jesus' invitation?
It is your decision, what will you do?
Revelation 3:20

I beg you be reconciled back to God
This is my earnest plea
Be saved from the consequences of your sin
And let God do for you what it is that He has done for me
II Corinthians 5:20

Written for the Glory of God

Hebrews 7:25. Wherefore also He is able to save to the uttermost those drawing near to God through Him, always living for to intercede for them.

14. Be Calm

Has the joy diminished from your life?
Have you lost your curiosity?
Have you lost your wonder of adventure?
Have you lost your sense of discovery?

Curiosity is the basic state of a child's mind
Life is full of adventure for the young
Little people have an intense curiosity about the world around them
An immense hunger to learn and grow and just have fun

Do not always be looking for the bad in life
Take time to acknowledge what is good
You know there really are caring and compassionate people
Scattered throughout the neighborhood

By the time we reach adulthood
We often become overly cautious and suspicious
Lose our taste for the simple pleasures in life
Where nothing seems appealing or delicious

If we spend too much of our time and energy
Trying to control and run the universe
Instead of finding joy and contentment
Things will just go from bad to worse

That is why we need to embrace the priceless gift of faith
And ask God to restore that childhood treasure once again
And not lean upon our own understanding
And let our kite fly freely in the wind
Proverbs 3:5

I am not saying we should embrace foolish gullibility
Or set aside all our responsibilities
But trust more in our heavenly Father
Spend more time in His Word and on our knees
John 14:1

We need to look to the One who created the heavens
The One who put each star in place
The One who hangs the moon and stars on nothing
As they orbit effortlessly in space
Isaiah 40:26; Job 26:7

We need to realize that trust, like joy, is an attitude
An attitude we can choose to embrace
We need to set on our heavenly Fathers knee so to speak
And once again look into His face

But you say, God is not a physical human being
Your words to my ears seem rather odd
How can you speak of such close intimacy?
When you speak of an invisible God

Poems Of Inspiration

You see, the Bible says faith comes through hearing the message
And the message is heard through the Word
And this message points us to the person and work of Jesus
But in today's churches its seldom heard
Romans 10:17

Can we not talk to friends and loved ones?
Those whom we cannot touch or see
Even if they are halfway around the world
Communicating to someone afar off is not a mystery

We can even talk to men and woman
Those who are far off in space
And because of modern technology
We can even see the image of their face

You see, God wants a close and intimate relationship
With each and every one of us
But most are caught up in the turmoil of this world
Of all the clamor, bustle and fuss

And sadly, the same can be said of those in the church
Of those caught up in ministry
From time to time, we need to examine ourselves
I know that this is true of me

There are so many things to discover
If we would simply spend time with Him
If we would spend time in God's Word and at the feet of Jesus
Take time out of our busy lives for the two of them
Luke 10:39

You know, God's Word is filled with commandments
We are commanded to love Him with all our heart
With all our mind and soul and strength
And each day comes with a fresh and brand-new start
Mark 12:30-31; Matthew 6:34

You are the Salt of the Earth

We can choose to trust that things will work out
And chances are, they will
So, if you are filled with anxiousness and apprehension
You need to hear the words "Be still"
Philippians 4:6-7; Psalm 46

The world is like a perilous sea with treacherous waters
It wants to hold you in a grip of fear
Satan wants you to dwell upon your past
Distract you by keeping your focus on the rearview mirror

Or he wants you to be fearful of the future
He wants to cloud your mind with uncertainty and doubt
He wants to fill you with a sense of hopelessness
Keep you in a pit and make you think there is no way out

He wants you to be fearful and ineffective
He wants anxiety to keep you unproductive
He wants you to be unfruitful in God's Kingdom
His purposes are always meant to be destructive

But when we are still and draw near to God
And more fully realize His supremacy
The dark waters and waves will be replaced with calm
With peace and quiet and tranquility

Jesus said we should look at the birds of the air
And that we should set aside some time
To set at His feet and learn to listen
By so doing it will give us peace of mind

Metaphorically, we do not see birds wringing their hands in anxiousness
They are not overwhelmed with care
We need to meet Him in the secret place
And spend time with Him there

We can learn to trust God for our daily needs
The One who set the stars in space
We need to daily come into His presence
And walk at a slower pace

He wants us to look at all of nature
He does not want our hearts to be filled with worry
He said look at the lilies of the field
He wants us to slow down and not always be in such a hurry

You are much more valuable than the lilies
And though the sparrows have a special place
Life for them is not a contest
Their lives are not a competition or a race

Come aside and find something fun to do
Do not let guilt be the master of your soul
Find a hobby or exercise and learn to be creative
Let balance be your friend and be your goal

Take time out of your busy schedule
Set aside some time to rest
You may find that it is rejuvenating
You may find that is when you are at your best

Satan is the author of confusion
The author of chaos and disorder
Jesus wants to calm the turmoil and turbulence
Maybe it is time for you to reverse the order

Jesus said come to me you who are burdened
Set at my feet if you want what is best
Come to me you who are weary
And I will give you rest

Written for the Glory God

15. Depart from me, Lord, I am a sinful man?

Oh, Theodore is such a good man
Do you see how he treats his wife?
How he always holds her hand in public
How he treats her so kind and nice

Theodore is also good with young children
And he so boldly speaks the truth
And when asked he does not hesitate
To help with the all-niter's with the youth

Theodore also visits the elderly in the nursing homes
And he does so many other goods things too
Yes, you can tell that he is a good man
By all the good things we see he is quick to do

And Theodore also teaches Sunday school
And he writes letters to the editor and other things
Even his voice sounds like it came from heaven
His voice is like an angel when he sings

And have you ever seen anyone so benevolent with his money?
And so generous with his time
And you will never hear a whimper come from the lips
of Theodore
Because he never grumbles, nor does he whine

He also works hard on outreach programs
And you can tell that he is a man of prayer
And by all his acts of kindness
You can see that he is a person who likes to share

And his prayers, why, they are just like flowers
Their scented fragrance fills the room
They are so elegant and impressive
Like the lilacs in spring when in full bloom

He never denigrates or belittles others
He always has something nice to say
And when he is in a group setting
It always brightens everybody's day

And Theodore always seems so cheerful
He is never impatient or in a hurry
He seems to overflow with confidence
He never seems to be concerned or worried

By now you might get the idea that Theodore is perfect
Did you know that he even helps around the house?
Thinking that he is as a good person that there could possibly be
That he is even a perfect spouse

You would almost think that he was sinless
Why, you might even think that he was God Himself
But if you want an honest evaluation of Theodore
Take your Bible off the shelf!!

You are the Salt of the Earth

You see, I am a sinful man
A man in need of God's amazing grace
And the same can be said of you
Since you are a part of the human race

This poem is about me and some of my struggles
But I hope that it will make you think
About humanity in general
That we are all on a spiritual boat that is doomed to sink

If you want to get a good look at ugly
Take a real close look at me
I am not talking about my outward appearance
Look inside what do you see?

For there is nothing that is more ugly
Then the ugliness of sin
The ugliness of sinful heart
That is rooted deep within

As you take the time to read this poem
You may see things that have been previously hidden from your sight
Some of the darker things that aren't so pretty
Things revealed to you once they have been brought into the light
I Corinthians 3:10-15

At times Theodore had some of these aforementioned qualities
And not all the things he did were always bad
But when you start to get a good look into the heart of Theodore
What you will see there is really kind of sad
II Timothy 3:5

You see, it is not we who set the standards
It is not we who standardize
And the Scriptures make it clear that God's standard is perfection
And for His standard He does not apologize
Revelation 21:27

You will find that Theodore wasn't very much like God at all
At least he didn't have many godly traits until he was "born again"
Before he accepted Jesus Christ into his life
And turned away from blatant sin
John 3:1-21; Hebrews 10:26-27

And even then, it has been and still is a journey
A process that at times seems so very slow
As I strive to grow in holiness as I follow Jesus
Now having an eternal perspective and an eternal goal
II Peter 1:5; Acts 24:16; Philippians 3:12-14

As we open up the Word of God
We find that God knows the beginning through the end
That He knows every thought we have ever thought
He knows our each and every sin
Revelation 22:13; Luke 9:47

He knows all the times he made his wife cry
Even though that has been a long time ago
You might start seeing a different side of Theodore
A private side of him you did not know
Ephesians 5:25

There were times I left my wife crying on the inside
When there were no outward tears for one to see
How easily we can hide and mask our hurt from others
And yet it was ongoing grace she has offered me

He knows all the times Theodore has been ill-mannered
All the times he has been rude and impolite
He knows all the times he has done the wrong things
Things in his heart that he knew were not right
I Corinthians 13:5; James 4:17

I indulged in pornography for a time
For a time, it was arousing and inviting
It stimulated all my brazen senses
For a time, it was exciting

But pornography is addictive
Like King Midas and his gold
It destroys people and relationships
Leaving a soul barren, lifeless and cold

I remember all the times I raised my voice in anger
And all the time's that I would withdraw and pout
A grown man acting very childish
Yes, He knows me inside out
I Corinthians 13:11

God knows of all the "planks" I have had in my eyes
While looking to remove the "specks" from the eyes of my Christian brothers
Since then, I have removed many planks from my eyes to see more clearly
Maybe now I can help remove the specks from others
Matthew 7:5

He knows all the time's that I kept records
All the times I held a grudge
When I would not reason or give in an inch
Like a stubborn mule that would not budge
I Corinthians 13:5

The Bible is clear that God hates divorce
Yet how many have divorced themselves from God
Never really having been His bride in the first place
Trampling His grace beneath the sod
Revelation 19:7-9; 1st John 2:19; Hebrews 10:29

Divorce is not the unpardonable sin
But why do so many choose this course?
Because all of us have sinful character flaws
When left unresolved sometimes lead to divorce

He knows all the time's when Theodore would throw a party
for himself
Parties that was far from being pretty
Narcissistic parties where no one else was invited
Where he waddled in a pool of his own self pity

God knows each one of Theodore's offenses
Each time he used vulgarity and swore
Every time lust welled up inside of his sinful heart
All his ungodly thoughts and so much more
Matthew 12:36; Colossians 3:8; Matthew 5:28

He knows each time Theodore lied and cheated
Each time he used an untruth to get himself out of a bind
Each time he stole from someone else
Yes, He knows his every crime
Leviticus 19:11

He knows all the time's that Theodore
Neglected to spend time in His Word
Even after going to church each week
Acting as if he had not heard
Matthew 4:4; James 1:22

He knows each time Theodore was proud and arrogant
Each time he felt hatred in his heart from deep within
Each time he tried to manipulate others through deception
He knows his every sin
Proverbs 12:2; Romans 3:23; Matthew 5:21-22

He knows when Theodore has been angry and mean-spirited
All the times he did not do the things that he was told
He knows all the time's that he was cowardly
He knows all the time's when his heart was hard and cold
Colossians 3:8

He knows all the time's Theodore has been indifferent
All the time's he was greedy and did not share
All the time's that he was apathetic
All the time's he simply did not care
Revelation 3:15

He knows all the time's Theodore had shown favoritism
All the times he had shown partiality
All the times he had looked at the specks in other's eyes
While the planks in his own eyes he could not see
James 2:1-13; Matthew 7:1-6

He knows when Theodore did not stand up for the truth
When he took credit for thing's he didn't do
Yes, He knows each dark secret in his heart
Not a single one is hidden from His view

He knows all the time's Theodore doubted Him
All the time's Theodore's heart was filled with anxiety and so much more
All the time's Theodore grumbled and complained
All the dark dismal things that are hidden behind the door
John 20:24-27; Philippians 4:6; James 5:9

Let us stop and pause for a moment
Let us make some comparisons with a book
It might help put things in perspective
If we take an honest look

Books do not just magically appear
There is more to a book than meets the eye
Many exceptional books have been written to bring God glory
And there are many books written based upon a lie

Proof reading and editing need to be done
Insights from others are often needed
Some errors may be found and corrected
And advice from others may need to be heeded

The Lambs book of life

My prayer is that your name will be found written in the
Book of Life
That you will escape the wrath to come
That you will be clothed in God's white raiment of righteousness
Provided by Jesus God's Only begotten Son

In reality I didn't do all these ugly things
But a great number of them are true
But it just goes to show you cannot judge a "book" by its cover
That is true of me as well as you

Most books we read have chapters
Does not the life we live have chapters too
Yes, we go through different ages and different pages
Growing and maturing is a process we go through

But just like the books we read
Our lives have a beginning and an end
Not a single word written goes unnoticed
God knows every word on every page that is written within

Yes, if you open the "book" of Theodore's life
Look beyond the cover and see what is written there within
And if others were to look beyond the cover and look inside the
"book" of your life
On the pages there would be a multitude of sins
James 5:9; Psalm 130:3

Every person's "book" will be read at some future time
On that Great and dreadful Judgment Day
And judgment will be dealt according to what is written
within the pages
So, I ask, have your sins been washed away?
Revelation 3:5; Isaiah 1:18

The Great Author of life will make no errors
When He judges people's words and deeds
He knows the intent of every heart
He clearly sees the useless chaff and deadly weeds
Psalm 1; Matthew 13:24-30

The Bible demands universal attention
We need to heed its many claims
We would be wise to investigate the "I am" claims of Jesus
If we want to escape Hell's eternal flames
John 6:35; 8:12; 10:7,9; 10:11,14; 11:25; 14:6; 15:1,5

The overwhelming majority of Americans
Have in their possession this Holy Book
We need to approach it with reverence and an inquiring mind
We need to give it more than just a casual look

One would suppose that to know God would be to honor God
But there are those who know God and suppress the truth
The knowledge concerning God is available to all
But there are adults who purposely distort and conceal it
from our youth
Romans 1:18

But children do not remain children
And when they grow up, they have to make a choice
They can choose to seek God or reject Him
They can choose to listen to or reject His voice

When a person rejects God's light and revelation
The final outcome is that only darkness will remain
It is to reject the light revealed to us in Jesus
For salvation is found in no other name
Acts 4:12

It does not matter if you have memorized whole books
of the Bible
One can still be a hypocrite or a Pharisee
You see we can still be misguided and foolish
I know that at one time that was true of me
John 5:39

And God knows your heart also
It does not matter if you are a priest, a pastor or a preacher
Or if you have gone to a Christian college
Or if you are a well-dressed distinguished Sunday
school teacher

Do you believe in Heaven?
As revealed to us in God's Holy Word
And that to enter Heaven the standard is perfection
This truth so many have not heard
Hebrews 10:14; Revelation 21:27

Maybe you feel you meet God's standard of perfection
That you do not have a blemish of any kind
That you are spotless and clean without a single flaw
With no need to renew your mind
Proverbs 20:9; Romans 12:1-2

You are the Salt of the Earth

That when you stand before a Holy God
You will say I am not like others who are dirty and unclean
Say you have no need for Jesus' redemptive work
upon the cross
That you have no need to be redeemed
Luke 18:9-14

Or maybe you have embraced this silly idea
That all the good things you have done will outweigh your bad
That you will get another chance next time around
Such thinking is dangerous and beyond just being sad
Isaiah 64:6; Hebrews 9:27

Or maybe you think your good works will get you Heaven
Well, I hope you will think again
And that you would take heed to Jesus' words
When he says, "You must be born again"
Ephesians 2:8-9; John 3:1-21

If we could really see our heart the way God sees it
We would see we are not so good after all
That there is a little of Adam and Eve in each one of us
That we have all been affected by the Fall
Jeremiah 17:9-10

Hell will be filled with a lot of good people
At least those who think themselves good in their own eyes
Those who are hardened to God's standard and compare themselves with others
Such comparisons are foolish and unwise
II Corinthians 10:12

But you, like Theodore can become a Christian
And a change in your heart, like Theodore's, can take place
And like him you can start getting victories over sins in your life
As you grow in God's benevolent grace
II Peter 3:18

Poems Of Inspiration

After becoming a Christian goodness started to take root
in Theodore
At times he truly was gentler and nice
He started to perform acts of kindness for God's glory
And he was gentler and more caring with his wife

If you were to put your name in the place of Theodore's
in this poem
What sins would be described in your "sin category"?
You see the list of sins is quite revealing
When you reflect what would be your "sin list" story?

Worried
Anger
Pride
Hate
Theft
Cowardliness
Rudeness
Swearing and vulgarity
Cheater
Ungodly thoughts
Liar
Irritability
Vindictive
Coveter
Lust…fornication…adultery…homosexuality
Greed
Indifference
Showing partiality
Manipulator
Grumbler…gossiper
Complainer
Jealousy
Envy…disobedience

Today, Theodore's past does not define him
These traits no longer characterize the way Theodore
strives to live
Where once Theodore was vindictive and vengeful
Theodore now has a heart's desire to share and to forgive
Acts 24:16

Theodore does not grumble as much as he used to
In fact, the positive traits you see in this poem
Today describes Theodore to some degree
As he continues his journey to his heavenly home
Philippians 3:20

You see, God's standard is perfection
And God Himself has made a way
And when Jesus died upon the cross
It was finished on that day
John 19:28-30; Revelation 21:27; I Peter 3:18

At least the atonement was finished
Forgiveness was made available for our sin
And after three days in the grave
Jesus defeated death and rose again
I Corinthians 15:3-4

Then He ascended into Heaven
This should give us comfort, peace and hope
That we can have confidence and assurance
Like when we hold firmly to a rope
Philippians 1:6

The rope that our God offers us
Is as simple as can be
It just takes a simple act of faith
And we can have eternal security

Poems Of Inspiration

Heaven and Hell hang in the balance
This is the most important decision a person will make
For one not to consider the implication of the Gospel
Would be a solemn and grave mistake
Joshua 24:15

The Gospel is both good news and a gracious offer
It is not something a person should scoff at or mock or laugh
It is not an offer a person should shun and turn from
For to do so one will remain under God's judgment
and His wrath
John 3:18

The Gospel message is inherently persuasive
Jesus calls all people to decide about Him
There is no getting around this
We can choose to repent or chose to remain in our sin
Matthew 16:13-20

We need to understand our sinfulness
And repent and turn from them
Turn from the darkness to the light
We need to follow Jesus-turn to Him
Romans 3:23; John 3:19-20

That does not mean we will not have problems
Or that we will not face turbulent trials
That this life will be free of suffering and excruciating pain
That life will always be a bowl of cherries accompanied
with smiles
I Peter 4:12

Life may be the very opposite
For Jesus said we all have a cross to carry
When Jesus was bludgeoned, beaten and spit upon before
her very eyes
Picture in your mind the heart of Mary

It should not be hard for any of us
To imagine what Mary must have been going through
Was this not a cross for Mary?
And each of us has a cross to carry too

You see, although you may not like the way it sounds
Outside of Christ all of us are "dirty and unclean"
As a result of the original sin in the Garden
That includes every single human being
Luke 18:11; Proverbs 30:12; Isaiah 64:6

And the only way one can be made clean and white as snow
Is to have our sin completely washed away
But in order for this to happen
An innocent and pure Lamb would have to pay
Isaiah 1:18

Look, the Lamb of God
The perfect Lamb that would give His life
He would take upon Himself the sins of all humanity
He was the perfect unblemished sacrifice
John 1:29

Since all of us stand guilty before a Holy God
We all fall into the category of being lost
And the only way we can be justified
Is to accept Jesus and what He did upon the cross
Romans 4:1-8

Justification is a legal term taken from the courtrooms of the first century
Justification expresses the judicial action of God apart
From human merit according to which the guilty stand pardoned, acquitted and reinstated
In which the guilty are given a new slate and brand-new start

Very simply, it means to be declared "not guilty" by a judge
And his word is final and complete
In other words, the person who has been justified
Starts out with a clean and empty sheet
Romans 3:21-31

God as judge pronounces His decision
He calls out, "Not guilty", you are set free
I hope you can hear His tender voice
And from eternal damnation turn and flee
Revelation 3:20

Our lostness will not simply go away
It is like a malignant cancer in the soul
We may try to deny that it exists
But it will continue to fester and grow

Those ugly traits that I once embraced
I do not embrace them anymore
Yes, traces of them can still be seen
But they are no longer at the center of my core

Sadly, there will be a lot of "good" people who will not enter Heaven
And a lot of religious and well-respected people as well
Those who think they will gain entrance to heaven by their own merits
But they will be cast into the eternal flames of Hell

And there is no reason for you to be one of them
If you have read and reflected on this poem
Jesus said, "You must enter through the narrow gate"
If you want Heaven to be your eternal home
Matthew 7:13

For our God is an inviting God
The Bible is filled with His invitations from the beginning
to the end
The most gracious invitation ever offered
Is for man to repent and turn to Him
Matthew 18:3; Revelation 3:20

What will you do with Jesus Christ?
This is the most decisive question that can ever be
The most crucial question put to an individual
For his answer will determine his eternal destiny
Mark 8:29

Stop and think about it
If a person does not think he needs Jesus Christ
Then he thinks he can stand before a Holy God
On his own merits or from the "goodness" done in his own life
Isaiah 64:6

He is saying that he is just as "good" as Jesus
That he is just as "good" as Deity
Then you need to open your Bible
Open the Scriptures so that you can clearly see
Acts 17:11

I hope that this sermon has convicted you
That it has penetrated your sinful heart
That you would repent and turn to Jesus
And ask Him to give you a brand-new start

For at that very moment
A miraculous STANDING before God will take place
Like a newborn baby you will be welcomed into His family
Starting a new journey as you start to grow in His wisdom
and His grace
I Peter 2:2; II Peter 3:18

Poems Of Inspiration

How sad it is that in our church and other churches
throughout our land
People could be attending week after week
Without a clear understanding of the Gospel
Going home with no desire to ask and knock and seek
Matthew 7:7

May this poem be to you a warning
Like the ringing of a bell
That there is a day of judgment coming
That there is a real eternal Hell
Matthew 25:41

And the only way for one to enter Heaven
Is to put their faith in what Jesus Christ has done
For God so loved the world
That He gave His One and Only Son
John 3:16

The Gospel is the good news indeed the greatest news
That it must be announced to all
Such crucial news must be communicated accurately and
sensitively
So that those who hear its beckoning can respond to its
pressing call

Do a little self-evaluation
Have you ever told a lie?
Remember, nothing is hidden from our Omnipresent God
Nothing is concealed from His all-seeing eye
Proverbs 15:3; II Corinthians 13:5; II Peter 1:10-11

Now ponder and chew over the question
What does that make you out to be?
I know that it may sound a little nasty
But it makes you a liar just like me

You are the Salt of the Earth

Remember what I said earlier
About having planks in my own eye
Well, I would be lying once again
If I told you that I never told a lie

A lie is a lie no matter what its color
Be it a black lie or a white
A lie is a lie no matter how big or how little
When exposed to God's glory and His light

Have you ever stolen anything?
This is question number two
Maybe some cookies at home or something from work
When we steal what does that make me and you?

Doesn't that kind of remind you of Judas?
I know that it is kind of hard to say
When we steal something, it makes us thief's
We are lawbreakers in the eyes of the law at the end of the day

Have you ever lusted after someone of the opposite sex?
Jesus calls such an act adultery
Even if it only takes place inside the mind
And Sodom and Gomorrah and the sin of homosexuality
Matthew 5:28

That makes you and adulterer or an adulteress or a sodomite
Words swept under the rug in our churches today
There are unmarried couples living together who attend
our churches
Thinking that such a lifestyle is perfectly okay

But it is not okay in the eyes of a Holy God
And the Bible is very clear
Marriage should be honored by all and the marriage bed kept pure
Could it be that God's judgment is very near?
Hebrews 13:4

Have you ever used God's name as a swear word?
Or Jesus' name other than with reverence
Then like me that makes you a blasphemer
Are you starting to see the darkness of our decadence?
Exodus 20:7

If we really do a close examination
We all have sinned and fall short of the glory of God
Thinking one is good enough to meet up with His standards
Is faulty thinking and rather odd
Romans 3:23

Some residues of our sinful habits
Have a tendency to stick around
All one need do is to be followed throughout the week
For some flaws and blemishes to be found

I heard it said some time ago
Although God is concerned about our perfection
That He is more concerned about our spiritual growth
Not so much about our perfection but our direction

It is obvious that He is concerned about both
But balance is the vital key
As we continue on our journey
That is God's desire for you and me
Ecclesiastes 7:16

The heart is deceitfully and desperately wicked
And the Omnipotent God knows the heart
All the bad and offensive things we have ever done
But in His grace, He offers us a fresh and brand-new start
Jeremiah 17:9

Just one other nib-bit, some food for thought
The holiday "Good Friday", how did it come to be?
The ultimate sacrifice that Jesus gave upon the cross
This Holy Day was "Good" for you and me

It is good to have good morals
But having high morals does not make a person good
Jesus said there is no one good but God
But this truth today is so misunderstood
Luke 18:19

There are a lot of people who are atheists
Those who do a lot of great and wonderful things
These people would fall under the category of being a moralist
But they say they have no need to bow down to the King of kings
Philippians 2:10-11

Me, I no longer profess to be a good man
But I am declared righteous in God's sight
For my faith is in what Jesus did on my behalf
And I strive to walk in God's light
Romans 4:5-8; Acts 24:16

And you, do you consider yourself to be a good person?
Or have you come to realize?
That maybe you are not so good after all
Now able to see through your self-deception and these cultural lies

Do you have unresolved anger in your life?
Maybe a seed of bitterness has taken root in your heart so long ago
Bitterness that has never been dealt with
Seeds planted deep cannot help but produce fruit and grow

Children who have been bullied and mistreated
Or who did not or do not have loving parents in the home
Where there is no balance of love and discipline
Or where they are simply neglected and left alone

Children that have had ungodly seeds planted within their heart
Seeds producing smoldering wicks and bruised reeds
Producing mistrust, fear, doubt and suspicion
These traits are caused by these deadly seeds
Isaiah 42:3; Matthew 12:20

The seed of self-pity can easily take root in these children
But there will come a time and place
As they grow older to choose to remain in it
Or choose to embrace God's grace

Maybe its time to forgive your parents or stepparents
Or anyone else who has hurt you in the past
No, it is true that they do not deserve your forgiveness
Maybe you are reasoning in your mind, besides, they did not ask

Forgiveness is a precious gift
And the deadly seeds need to be replaced
Reflect on God's mercy and grace on your behalf
His special gift of forgiveness for sinners needs to be embraced

We live in a dark and fallen sinful world
Like DNA sin is imprinted on the human heart
How often we ourselves need forgiveness
For inner healing forgiveness is where we need to start

My father was an alcoholic
His father was an alcoholic too
What about his father and grandfather?
To be honest I haven't got a clue

But the chain of mistrust and fear can be broken
Jesus said a change can take place within the heart
We ourselves can become a part of God's family
Forgiveness is the place to start
Ezekiel Chapter 18

Forgiveness truly is a gift
It cannot be merited or earned
Look at all the sinful traits mentioned earlier
There's room for all of us to grow and learn

Jeremiah was right in His observation about the human heart
And so was the Apostle Paul
When he said, "There is no one who is good"
That we are sinners one and all
Jeremiah 17:9; Romans 3:9-18

All of us need to come face to face with this reality
That we fall short of God's standard of perfection
That the sanctification process is always ongoing
That we need to follow God's compass to lead us in the right direction
Romans 3:23; II Peter 1:3-11

God's purpose is not just to save us from Hell
Although that is indeed a wonderful thing
But for all of us to dwell on the splendor of Jesus
And the restoration and healing He longs to bring
Matthew 11:11-28

All of us should have a desire to mature spiritually
To love God and walk in the beauty of His power
To be educated in the knowledge and grace found in Jesus
O, how much this education is needed in this dark hour
Matthew 5:6; II Peter 3:18

To learn to understand His grace is no longer about trying harder
Or to simply quit doing the sinful things we do
But that it is about walking in the newness of life
That is God's desire for me and you

As we grow in the process of sanctification
Our worldly desires will gradually pass away
As we learn to spend time at the feet of Jesus
We will find that it truly is the better way
Luke 10:38-42

We will learn to love God more than we love our sin
And though no discipline seems pleasant at the time
Eventually it will produce a harvest of righteousness
Growing in grace will lead to peace of mind
Hebrews 12:11

Living for God isn't a partial commitment
It is a daily devotion that requires our time
It involves prayer and reading and meditating on His Word
This will bring forth fruit in the renewing of our mind
John 15; Romans 12:1-2

When we hurt someone we love we apologize
And do we not desire to spend time with the people we love
The same holds true in our relationship with our
Heavenly Father
As we set our hearts and minds on thing above
Colossians 3:1-2

Me, I am still a work in progress
But I now have an eternal purpose and a goal
My prayer is that you too will join me on my journey to Heaven
That you will consider the destiny of your soul
Philippians 3:13-14

Written for the Glory of God

The "I" in this poem is me. Please take the time to look up and read the referenced Scriptures.

Ecclesiastes 7:16-17. Do not be over righteous, neither be over-wise! Why destroy yourself? Do not be overwicked, and do not be a fool! Why die before your time? It is good to grasp the one and not let go of the other. The man who fears God will avoid all extremes.

II Timothy 3:16. All Scripture is God-breathed and is useful for teaching, rebuking, correcting and training in righteousness.

Luke 5:8. But when Simon Peter saw it. He fell down before Jesus, saying, depart from me; for I am a sinful man, O Lord.

16. You can be Sure

*1st John 5:13 "I write these things to you who believe in the
name of the Son of God
so that you may know that you have eternal life."*

Do we not all want boundaries in our lives?
Boundaries that give us a semblance of sanity
That gives of some confidence amongst the chaos
Amongst the confusion and deception in our society

Boundaries are important in order to have peace of mind
They give us a sense of security
How much more concern we should have for our eternal soul
To know where we will spend eternity
1st John 5:13

Children live in a land of make-believe
In a land where they will never grow old and die
Where they dream of a paradise of exquisite beauty
Where the sun always shines, and they can fly

As an adult reflect on your childhood
Do not these words ring true?
You had no concept of time and eternity
For most, maybe that is not true of you

But as children grow up dark clouds blot out the sun
And their dreamlike land evaporates in thin air
The harsh realities of fallen humanity appear on the horizon
They discover that life is often so unfair

Instead of soaring on wings above the forested hills
They find they are unable to get off the ground
Like a kite closeted and still hidden in its package
A flightless kite shackled and bound

Children often struggle with insecurities
Children often do things they should not do
They are in need of our love and our instruction
Not condemnation from me or you

This is also true for the children of God
So often we are frail and weak
We too often struggle with insecurities
That is why Jesus said we are to ask and knock and seek
Matthew 7:7

If some are honest, they have a plastic faith
A faith that is brittle and breakable
The foundation beneath them is like that of shifting sand
Stunting their ability to mature and grow
II Peter 1:5; Matthew 7:24-26

Have you ever struggled with uncertainties?
Had an inner battle in your soul
Been uncertain and insecure in your salvation?
Have you had doubts and said, "I do not know"?

Some honestly struggle with the question
"Can a person really know"?
Can a person really be certain about Heaven?
That upon their death that is where they will go

Poems Of Inspiration

We need to examine ourselves from time to time
Why not take the time to look up the word "deceive"
Ask ourselves "Is there such a thing as "absolutes"?
Ask ourselves "What is it we really believe"?
1st Corinthians 11:28

Sadly, some Christians are saved but almost fruitless
This is indeed a sad commentary
A neglect to invest in gold, silver and costly stones
Is not the thought of surviving through burning stubble
kind of scary?
1st Corinthians 3:12

Some argue, a Christian cannot be fruitless!
With you the apostle Paul would disagree
And besides, I did not say fruitless I said "almost"
When we read, we need to read carefully

Even among those who sit in our churches today
There are those who are uncertain of what they believe
And there are those who are confident in their own goodness
Sadly, there are multitudes sitting in churches that are deceived
Luke 18:9; Matthew 7:23

And there are those who have honest struggles
Those who are sincere in their search for the truth
Because of all the spiritual deception around them creating confusion
Deception that is having a strong influence upon our youth
Mark 9:24

When you hear devastating news that shatters your world
When the darkness wants to blind you and steal away your light
God's promises will resurface in your mind and will remind you
And help renew your spirit and your sight

Truth, love, mercy, grace
Balance is the vital key
Teaching from behind the pulpit
And our own responsibility

Thomas's slowness and backwardness to believe
Is revealed in Scriptures for a reason
They are there for those of us who struggle at times with doubt
Even those "sealed" in Christ may have doubt that lingers for a season
Ephesians 1:13; John 20:25

We can be certain in Christ's Deity—-that He is God
Not a man-made God, but God the Creator who made man
We can know and sing with confidence
"On Christ this Solid Rock I Stand"
John 1:1-4; 14:9; Matthew 1:22-23

Doubt can thrust us into a deeper self-search for certainty
And put a hunger and thirst within our soul
Help us develop a more intimate relationship with Jesus
At the end of our search, we can proclaim with confidence "I know"
Matthew 5:6

Life, death, and eternity
Great faith issues worth struggling through
We can have a strong faith built upon a solid foundation
A blind faith need not be said of me or you
Hebrews 9:27; 1st Corinthians 3:10-15

Like Thomas, we can cry out, "My Lord and my God"
Because of all the overwhelming evidence
We can worship Him in truth and in Spirit
And serve Him with confidence
John 20:28; Romans 1:20; John 4:23

Doubting is not a curse as many think
It is often a blessing in disguise
Planting within us a desire for knowing and experiencing God
Although this will require a little spiritual exercise
Psalm 25:4-7

"Blessed Assurance" is available to all of us
The promises are found in God's most Holy Book
It can be experienced and authenticated
So, come with me and take a look
1st John 5:13

We desire certitudes in the life we live
Life is too precious to live haphazardly
Life demands that we make plans and preparations
We should not live life ignorantly or unintentionally
Matthew 7:24

Yes, God has placed before us some boundaries
Boundaries that bring blessings for you and me
We see the consequences where they are missing
We understand the importance of laws in society

There are many who know Bible doctrines
There are some that are hardcore fundamentalists
They know the rules the dos and don'ts
They have their check off boxes and their lists
John 5:39

And then there are those who are ignorant of basic
Bible doctrines
They float along and say "All you need is love"
They never take the time to ask and knock and seek
Or set their hearts and minds on the things above
Hebrews 5:12; Matthew 7:7; Colossians 3:1

We do not expect our children to remain children
We come alongside them and teach them as they
mature and grow
We teach them by example, and we love them
We teach them that we reap just what we sow
Deuteronomy 6:6-7; Galatians 6:7

Child development comes with many struggles
And spiritually that is true of those who have been "born again"
We understand that the sanctifying process is progressive
As we face the storms, the rain, the wind
John 3:3; II Peter 1:5; Matthew 7:25

Growing pains are experienced by children
They are indeed a reality
And spiritual growth this truth applies as well
At least it has been true of me

What does it mean to be a Christian?
A Christian is one who grows in grace
It is one who grows in the knowledge of our Lord and Savior
A Christian is one who takes the time to seek His face
Acts 11:20-21; II Peter 3:18; Psalm 27:8

We can have confidence to enter the Most Holy Place
Jesus has opened for us a way
So, let us draw near to God with a sincere heart
In full assurance of faith when we pray
Hebrews 10:19-22

Having had our hearts sprinkled to cleanse us of a guilty
conscience
His grace allows us to have peace of mind
And having had our bodies washed with pure water
Our confidence will grow with the passing of time
Hebrews 10:22

Yet at times the weakness of our flesh will surface
At such times we need to lift our soul to Him
We must pray for His great mercy and love
And receive His promise to pardon our sin
Psalm 25:4-7; 1st John 1:9

For we have many enemies in this life
Enemies from without and from within
This world's system as well as the demonic
And with our own flesh we must contend
Romans 7:15-25

Some skeptics mockingly ask the question
Why does this alleged God hide in secrecy?
If He is real, why doesn't He step out in the open?
So that all can clearly see
Matthew 16:4

Why doesn't He step out on center stage?
Why does He shroud Himself in mystery?
If He is the God that you say He is
Provide me with evidence so I can see

But God has indeed stepped out on center stage
When God Himself shared in our humanity
Read John chapter one verse fourteen
And John chapter one verses one through three

We must remember that sanctification is an ongoing process
And that we will face many battles in this life
Remember Peter when he looked at the turmoil about him
Having taken his eyes off Jesus Christ
Ephesians 6:10-18; Matthew 14:30

At times we too have storms raging around us
We too find our ship in the midst of the sea
How often in storms my faith would quickly weaken
Replaced with fear that would well up in me
Matthew 7:24

And often it is and has been my own weaknesses
That causes my fear and doubt
But it is the faithfulness of Christ and his secure hand
And my taking it that leads me out
1st Corinthians 1:8-9; John 10:28-30

It is no new thing for the followers of Christ
To meet with storms along the way
Though troubles and difficulties may disturb us
They should make us more earnest when we pray
John 16:33

As a child one may have an innocent childlike faith
A faith built on what others believe
But growing older and experiencing hardships and trials
One might start to question as to whether he was deceived

A faith built on what others believe can be shattered
When one faces severe trials in this life
Hopefully making one come to terms and examine himself
As to what he really believes about Jesus Christ
II Corinthians 13:5; II Peter 1:10-11

When one sees the human weaknesses of those in the church
And one's own weaknesses and sin
He may doubt himself and ask the question
Have I truly been born again?
John Chapter 3

Personal questions will accompany us on our journey
In our heart and mind, they will arise
As we observe all the inequities in this life
As we battle against our own flesh and Satan's lies

When you start to base your assurance on your performance
On how well or on how poorly that you or others do
You have taken your eyes off from Jesus
And what it is that He has done for you
1st Peter 3:18

Your personal pilgrimage can give you the "Blessed Assurance"
If you learn to listen to this God who speaks
Salvation is a gift bestowed on the vilest of sinners
On the one who earnestly in his heart truly seeks
Matthew 7:7-8; Luke 18:9-14

The book of Hebrews declares two great facts
There is a God, and he is a God who speaks
And in the last days he has spoken to us by his Son
He readily speaks to the one who seeks
Hebrews 1:1-4

Modern man with all his worldly intelligence
Is unable to arrive at the knowledge of the truth
They have successfully removed God from our public schools
And teach a secular philosophy to our youth
1st Corinthians 3:18-20

They say we are but the outcome of accidental collocations of atoms
And they embrace an "eat drink and be merry" mentality
They have no moral standard of absolutes
They say to themselves I will have no God ruling over me
Luke 12:19; 1st Corinthians 15:32

They say we all are destined to extinction
That all man's achievements come to nothing
That they will not be held accountable for their actions
Crowning and proclaiming they themselves to be king
Matthew 12:36; Judges 21:25

In a world of modern technology and development
Such knowledge leaves behind a sad commentary
For many they have lost meaning and purpose for life
Embracing such a philosophy is not only sad but scary

The more they become aware of the intricacy of the universe
The less their sense of an overriding purpose and cause
Instead of believing in the Christ of Christmas
They embrace the philosophy of Santa Clause

The more they master the details of nature and the heavens
The more they lose sight of the reality
Of the great genius behind the creation
And the purpose of Calvary
1st Corinthians 1:18-31

With their God-given ability to study the universe
They have concluded we are a result of an accident
Their great knowledge leaves no room for God
Casting him aside as a worthless piece of lent
Psalm 14:1

Using human reasoning as their scaffolding
They build on a foundation frail and weak
They study the creation but reject the Creator
They refuse to ask and knock and seek

Poems Of Inspiration

On such a weak and faulty foundation
Their house will ultimately crumble and fall
Even childhood stories expose their foolishness
Were there not consequences when Humpty Dumpty fell off the wall?
1st Corinthians 10:12

Such assurance does not diminish the cost of discipleship
Nor does it eliminate the temptation to sin
Or the temptation to be apathetic or indifferent
Or neglect one's responsibility to spiritual discipline

Nor does it diminish the possibility of persecution
Or of personal suffering
Yet nothing can separate us from the love of our Heavenly Father
Or from Jesus this great yet humble King
Romans 8:35; Philippians 2:6-8

It is only in Christ such assurance is possible
This is an assurance on which we can depend
Even when our feelings are at their lowest ebb and when faith falters
We can depend on the faithfulness of Him
Hebrews 13:8; 1st Corinthians 1:8-9

We can be sure that God will not fail us
His promises are true because He stands behind each one
We see this in the birth, death, and resurrection of Jesus
God's gift to us is the person of His Son
Hebrews 6:18; 1st Corinthians 15:3-4

What are some of the reasons that we doubt?
Some come from without some come from within
Sometimes the accusing accusations of the devil
Causes us to doubt that we were "born again"
Revelation 12:10

All of us have been tempted to do something wrong or something foolish
Being tempted in and of itself is not a sin
When tempted we have a choice to make
Whether to refrain or to give in

Sometimes we make the right choice
And we gain the victory
But not in each and every situation
Sometimes we fail miserably

We sin in big ways and in little ways
Sometimes we commit what is known as sins of omission
Sometimes we sin by doing what we should not do
These are what are known as sins of commission

But that is not true of Jesus
He was and is the Perfect Spotless Lamb
The Lamb that would take away the sins of the world
Indeed, He was and is the Great "I AM"

A Christian will never attain sinless perfection
Who of us can claim to be sinless?
That is why the doctrine of sanctification is so important
A process as we are growing, we will sin less and less
Proverbs 20:9; Leviticus 11:44; II Peter 1:5

We can come into God's presence unashamedly
Not because of any good works that we have done
Not because of any righteousness of our own
But by our faith in Christ, God's Only Begotten Son
Philippians 3:9; Isaiah 64:6

Do we not draw near to those we love?
Our Heavenly Father's desire is that we draw near
Our faith is in Him and His unchanging character
We can approach Him with confidence and without fear
James 4:8; Hebrews 6:18

Our faith experience is interrelational
A relationship with our Heavenly Father and His Son
It is not based on our feelings, creeds or in our disciplines
But on our behalf what Christ has done
John 14:9; 1st Peter 3:18

Do not let the enemy of your soul deceive you
No longer allow him to blind you to the truth
Educating yourself is of utmost importance
Before you can pass on what you know to our youth
Romans 2:21

To strengthen your grasp on this blessed assurance
Take the time memorize a verse or two
Understand your sin nature and God's mercy and grace
Meditate on what it is that God has done for you
Proverbs 22:17-18; Romans 6:23

Earlier I mentioned "absolutes"
But I think it is important that I mention them again
God's Word says salvation is a gift offered to repentant sinners
And on His Word, we can depend
Matthew 24:35

How many times have you questioned God's reality?
Because of the circumstances you were in?
Circumstances you had very little control of
Where the ice beneath your feet seemed very thin

God has revealed Himself to all men
This is known as general revelation
The genius behind every created thing
The ingenuity and brilliance of creation clearly points to Him
Psalm 19; Romans 1:20

God spoke the universe into existence
He brought the galaxies into being
He brought into being the miracle of the human mind
His divine power is clearly seen
Genesis 1:3, 6, 9, 11, 14, 20, 24, 26, 29; Romans 1:20

One must willfully reject the evidence
To make the foolish claim that God does not exist
Willingly shut their eyes and close their ears
And in their heart purposefully resist
Romans 1:20; Psalm 14:1; Jeremiah 5:21

Creation declares God's supremacy and authority
The heavens declare His glory
But God wants us to know Him as a friend
And thus, we have the Gospel story
Psalm 19; John 15:15

We see in the earliest accounts of Genesis
That God walked in relationship with Adam and Eve
And we see Satan enter the picture as well
With his purpose and motive to deceive
Genesis 3:8; Genesis 3:1

Satan was not interested in intimacy and friendship
But God walked with Adam and Eve in the cool of the day
Before sin there was peace and harmony in the Garden
Before Satan lead the two astray

Poems Of Inspiration

Close fellowship with God was broken
When man chose to listen to the devil's voice
Replacing close intimacy with guilt and shame
Followed by the consequences of his choice

We must not lean upon our own understanding
But trust in God's reliability
For He is knowable and reliable
This God of time and history
Proverbs 3:5

God is still speaking as in days of old
Just as He has been throughout the ages
His full revelation is found in the Bible
Truth is revealed throughout its pages

Integrity of exploration is integral to Christian faith
Jesus destroys the concept of "blind faith" to those who seek
God desires that we exercise our free will and intellect
He does not want us to be ignorant or spiritually weak
Matthew 7:7; Luke 10:27; Hebrews 12:12

There are many things we may need not to be sure of
But it is essential that we know
About eternity, Heaven and Hell
And where it is that we will go

And what it means to be separated from God
And what it means to be "born again"
What it means for one to be dead in their transgressions
And that there are eternal consequences for our sin
Isaiah 59:2; John Chapter 3; Ephesians 2:1; Romans 6:23

God's Word is much more than a religious "best seller"
The Bible is an expression of divinity
Meaning that it came forth from the very God of Heaven
Within it His grace is freely offered to you and me
II Timothy 3:16-17

God's love came down from Heaven
Clothed in the person of His Son
Right before He breathed His final breath made this pronouncement
It is finished it is done
John 19:28-30

God's self-revelation in the person of Christ
Is a personal message of love
More than all the Old Testament prophetic announcements
More than all the angelic pronouncements from above
Matthew 1:23; Hebrews 1:1-2

Right from the very beginning
We see a prophecy about God's Son
And the shedding of innocent blood for forgiveness
That ultimately would be fulfilled in this Holy One
Genesis 3:15; Genesis 3:21

Blood was shed that a covering might be made
For our failure due to sin
Did not Jesus eat with tax collectors and sinners?
All he asks is that you invite him in
Genesis 3:21; Mark 2:15-22; Revelation 3:20

For those who feel themselves unworthy
They have their eyes fixed in the wrong place
Revealed in the Scriptures is the love of God
And His amazing gift of grace
Ephesians 2:8

Poems Of Inspiration

Jesus said, "Blessed are those who hunger and thirst for righteousness"
Jesus said, "Man does not live on bread alone"
"Behold, I have inscribed you in the palms of my hands"
The Lord desires to call each of us His very own
Matthew 5:6; Matthew 4:4; Isaiah 49:16; II Peter 3:9

For those of us who are painfully aware of our sin nature
Our response to God's love may be rather slow
His promises and pursuit are not thwarted by our slowness
He promises to never let us go
Hebrews 13:5-6

I personally embraced a sinful lifestyle
I chose to dwell in the city of sin
And I tried to drown my pain and anguish of my life
I chose to allow self-pity to dwell within

Alcohol was my drug of choice
I did not seek out love and intimacy
I looked for purpose in all the wrong places
One was my addiction to pornography

God seeks those wandering in the wilderness
With His invitation for us enter the "Promise Land"
And for those who accept Jesus' gracious invitation
No one can snatch them out of His or His Father's hand
Exodus 4:27; Deuteronomy 1:19-45; Revelation 3:20; John 10:28

The self-righteous Pharisees rejected His invitation
The door of their hearts was closed to him
They looked down on and judged the followers of Jesus
Metaphorically speaking they had "no room for him in the inn"
John 9:34; Luke 2:7

God's love is everlasting
And nothing can separate us from his love
Neither death nor life nor demons
We are sealed by him who sits enthroned above
Jeremiah 31:3 Romans 8:37-39; Ephesians 1:13

His assurance is given in his Word
His love toward us it is not forced
By some outside powers but freely given
It is willful, decisive and not coerced

God's love is the ultimate sacrificial love
A humble love of serving and suffering
And sinful man is the object of his love
With its offer of salvation, it would bring

His love is like a bright light shinning in the darkness
Making all others pale in radiance
His love has overcome the darkness
We can approach him with confidence

God commits his love to us eternally
This love cannot be equated with human love
That often manipulates, dominates, and exploits for one's own selfish desires
God's love was demonstrated when Christ descended from above
Jeremiah 31:3

For God the Father gave His Only Begotten Son
For the Son of man came to seek and save the lost
While we were yet sinners Christ died for us
Our salvation came at the greatest cost
John 3:16; Luke 19:10; Romans 5:8

Poems Of Inspiration

No matter who you are or where you are
And no matter what evil you have done
God's grace is offered to the vilest of sinners
All one needs to do is to look to Jesus Christ God's Only Son

Today the church seems far removed
From tabernacles, priests, and sacrificial lambs
One may even question if the blood of Jesus is necessary
This ancient teaching from some far-off distant land
1st John 1:7

The blood sacrifices of the Old Testament were symbolic
Of the ultimate gift that was to come
The blood of bulls and goats could never cleanse us of our sin
It would take the blood of God's most precious Son
Hebrews 10:4

Our security is based on the divinely inspired Word of God
The Bible is our authority
God was preparing an everlasting sacrifice replacing all ancient traditions
When Jesus' blood was shed for you and me

You can be sure there is no remedy
For our imperfections and our sin
Except for the shed blood of Jesus on our behalf
All one need do is look to Him

God's love does not remove us from the possibility of suffering
From illness, discomfort, or agony or pain
But as we persevere through the trials and testing
We can grow stronger through the stress and strain
James 1:12

You are the Salt of the Earth

Scripture and historical experience have taught us
That we cannot be saved by living a moral life
We cannot be saved by joining a church or "quoting Scripture"
Our salvation takes a perfect sacrifice
John 5:39

But there are those who are protesting
You do not know all the vile things that I have done
The hateful thoughts and hurtful actions
That God would forgive each and everyone
1st Timothy 1:15

Great sinners embracing a great grace
Moses, King David and the Apostle Paul
Lest we forget or unaware
They were murderers one and all

Sometime the slow stain of sin has seeped in so deeply
So deeply into the soul we are unable to believe
That even God himself could forgive us
Such thinking only comes when we are deceived

Sin is when we willingly and knowingly do
The wrong things we commit
Sin is not doing the things we should do
The things we knowingly omit

As Christians we have the highest calling
Jesus used the illustration of the simple fisherman
One need not attend a school of higher learning
Or have a worldly education to understand

In fact, this world's wisdom is foolishness in the eyes of God
An ungodly system void of truth
With a foundation built on sinking sand
A system on which they indoctrinate our youth
1st Corinthians 3:18-20; Matthew 7:24-27

As for the education of our children
Satan has had great success
By replacing the once secure and solid foundation
With one unable to persevere under the stress

Why did Jesus come into the world?
It was not for vainglory or for fame
Where did his signs and wonders and miracles ultimately lead him?
Ultimately, he was exposed naked on a cross of shame
Luke 19:10; Matthew 20:28; Philippians 2:6-11

Do you need signs, wonders and miracles?
Is that what it takes for you to believe?
The Scriptures make it clear the Satan masquerades as an angel of light
His purpose and goal were and still is to deceive
II Corinthians 11:14; John 8:44

Do you need signs, wonders and miracles?
To help you believe and overcome your doubts?
The evidence and truth are so overwhelming
To an honest seeker the evidence literally shouts

The Scriptures make it clear that faith comes by hearing
And hearing by the Word of God
Today much of what is passed off as signs, wonders and miracles
Is no more than a superficial façade
Romans 10:17

It is regrettable that in some areas of our church life
We tend to judge spiritual success
On our feelings or mystical events that take place
And not by our faithfulness

Such is not the biblical criterion
By which we are to measure
Our spirituality or our faith
The Word of God should be our treasure

Faith is being sure of what we do not see
That is what the ancients were commended for
So, take the time to open your Bible
It is the key that unlocks the door
Hebrews 11:1-3

All the miracles recorded from the life of Jesus
Were only incidental to the real purpose of his ministry
The great things referred to extend beyond these happenings
Signs and wonders were immediate but only temporary
John 3:1-3

The miracles that Jesus preformed were side issues
For Jesus came to seek and save the world from sin
He flung the door of Heaven wide open
With an invitation to all to enter in
Revelation 3:20

You see, there is a greater thing than miracles
You ask, what could that be
It is when one believes on Jesus and receives the gift of eternal life
The gift that Jesus offers you and me

It is greater than spiritual gifts within the church
Such as the gift of prophesy
It is greater than the gift of tongues
Or the gift of giving generously
I Corinthians 13:2; I Corinthians 13:1; I Corinthians 13:3

Such gifts can often be disruptive
Can create confusion and disunity
Some may be accompanied with pride
Sadly, there were at times that that has been true of me
I Corinthians 14:23; I Corinthians 13:4

False prophets have at times infiltrated the church
And Satan masquerades as an agent of light
One is saved by faith and faith alone
It is important that we get this right
Matthew 7:15; II Corinthians 11:14; Ephesians 2:8; I Corinthians 15: 3-6; Proverbs 14:12

As Christians we should walk with a humble spirit
We are to set our hearts and minds on things above
And grow in the grace and knowledge of our Savior
As we learn to walk in love
Micah 6:8; Colossians 3:1-4; II Peter 3:18; Ephesians 5:2

It is sharing the Gospel message of salvation
It is pointing lost sinners to the cross
Jesus' miracles and wonders fade into the background
Jesus' main purpose was to come and seek those who were lost
1st Corinthians 13:1-13

Therefore, we read, "Anyone who has faith in me-
Will do what I have been doing...even greater things than these-
Because I am going to the Father"
The salvation message is greater than miracles and
healing a disease
John 14:12; Luke 17:11-12

Some residues of sin remain
Even for those who have been "born again"
But One's standing before the God of Heaven is perfect
At that very moment they trust in Jesus to cleanse them of their sin
Hebrews 10:14; Ephesians 1:13

We live in that blessed hope
But our humanness longs for certainty
That there is life beyond the grave
A secure place in Heaven for all eternity

We have that blessed assurance from the lips of Jesus
The One who said, "I am the resurrection and the life"
His resurrection validates and authenticates all his other claims
They come from the lips of the One who paid the ultimate sacrifice
John 11:25

Written for the Glory of God

Please take the time to read the Scriptures that are referenced in this poem

John 10:28-30. I give them eternal life, and they shall never perish, no one can snatch them out of my hand. My Father, who has given them to me, is greater than all, no one can snatch them out of my Father's hand. I and the Father are one.

Ephesians 1:13. And you also were included in Christ when you heard the truth, the gospel of your salvation. When you believed, you were marked in him with a seal, the promised Holy Spirit, who is a deposit guaranteeing our inheritance until the redemption Of those who are God's possession-to the praise of his glory.

17. Bugs and Things

Exploring nature is a wonderful experience
For we can discover God's creativity
The amazing and cunning masters of disguise
The magic of camouflage and mimicry

God made the delightful birds of Paradise
With beauty that is pleasing to our eyes
Our God is a specialist in diversity
He is not only creative but all-wise

Ah, God's amazing awesome creatures
He gave us bugs and things
Bugs that crawl and hop and climb
Dragonflies with amazing wings

Nature is filled with astonishing animals
With a large variety of creatures
Some bizarre and strange and weird
And each with their own distinctive features

Animals that cleverly disguise themselves
Masters at hiding in plain sight
And God gave us luminous creatures
That light up and shine at night

You are the Salt of the Earth

God made fish that lie in wait on the ocean floor
Those with a built-in fishing pole
Striking like a flash of lightning
Swallowing their unsuspecting victims whole

God has blessed mankind with many riches
Pearls and diamonds and precious metals
And he has blessed us with the amazing flower mantis
With wings shaped like flower petals

Some insects blend in with their surroundings
Others simply fool their enemies
Like spiders that look just like bird droppings
Hiding in plain view while sitting on some leaves

Some male grasshoppers sing a special song
By rubbing their wings against their legs
Just the right song the lady grasshopper needed
First comes serenading than the eggs

The puss moth caterpillar has a frightening face
On its wings it has great big staring eyes
These features frighten away its enemies
A very effective disguise

Although spiders do not have wings
Some can fly above the highest trees
Floating effortlessly while attached to a long silk thread
Carried along by a gentle breeze

Honeybees make us a delightful treat
Do you like the sweet taste of honey?
Well, you should look at the honey pot ant
If you want to see something strange and funny

God made spiders of different shapes and sizes
Some of them are a master of disguise
Some of them get as large as dinner plates
And God made some of them with great big eyes

There are spiders that mimic ants
And there are beautiful spiders too
There are 44 varieties of peacock spiders
Displaying their colors in the spectrum of their brilliant hue

God also made net-casting spiders
Yes, spiders come in such a large variety
And most are blessed with unique skills and abilities
Some have eight eyes so they can see

Spiting spiders have fangs that spit a deadly silk
You could say that they have a special skill
Silk that paralyzes their victims
Before they come in for the kill

God has made a large variety of spiders
The Goliath bird-eating spider can get as big as a dinner plate
And one must beware of the dreadful black widow
Infamous for her reputation of eating her mate

Yes, it is true that there are spitting spiders
And He made bird-eating spiders too
There are dancing spiders and venomous spiders
And a tarantula that has the pretty color cobalt blue

In the world of nature there is much beauty
And yet so much violence can be seen
Beautiful flowers and amazing animals
Poisonous plants and vicious animals cruel and mean

How would you like to have creepy-crawlies living on
your body?
It is true of slow moving three-toed sloths
They even have green algae growing on their fur
Making a nice home for beetles, flees and moths

Our God is awe-inspiring and amazing
All creation shows His awesome power
It can be seen in the precise clockwork of the universe
And in the beauty of the delicate pedals of a flower

It can be seen in dancing spiders
It can be seen in dancing bees
It can be seen in the many mysteries we find in nature
It can be seen in the depths of the oceans and the seas

Written for the Glory of God

18. Suffering

"Naked I came from my mother's womb
And naked I will depart"
These words spoken by Job were received as words of worship
From an aching and painful heart
Job 1:21

In his grief he sat among the ashes
Scraping his sores with a piece of broken pottery
The greatest example of suffering in the Old Testament
That has been placed before you and me

The book of Job probes basic questions
Questions that have troubled human beings from the beginning
"Why do the righteous suffer?"
Those who shun a life of blatant sinning

When we experience heartrending tragedy
The question may arise, "How can God be just?"
While the wicked prosper and delight in the downfall of
the righteous
Singing "Another one bites the dust"

Suffering comes in so many different forms
The question through the ages has been "Why?"
Why must we drink from the bitter cup of suffering?
And today many can relate to their anguish and their cry?

For some it is the dreaded news from a doctor's office
For some it is the abandonment of a spouse brought on
by divorce
Saying the "feelings" of love have long since faded
Breaking the marriage covenant, one chooses a different course

For some it is the heartache of a delinquent son or daughter
For some it is a loss of employment and financial stability
For some it is misunderstandings or false accusations
For some it is a death of a loved one in the family
Luke 15:11-32; Luke 3:14; John 11; Luke 7:11-17

Job was a man of great wealth with a gentle spirit
Job was an upright God-fearing man
Job was generous and benevolent
He was known for his kindness throughout the land
Job 1:3; Job 1:1

Job was a servant of the God of Heaven
He was considerate and polite
He had gained the respect and admiration of those
who knew him
He was known as one who walked in God's glorious light

Job's godliness was sincere and genuine
His moral character was honorable and upright
Though not sinless he did not dwell in the land of wickedness
His heart's desire was to walk in the light
Hebrews 10:26; 1st John 1:7

But Job's friends had a developed theology
In their eyes Job had committed some hideous sin
Why else would this misfortune have befallen him?
In their eyes his suffering all fell back on him
John 9:1-12

His hands had done no violence
His prayers were unadulterated and pure
Yet his friends said if he would acknowledge his wrongdoing
In that he would find the cure
Job 16:17

There is a lot of suffering in the world
One might well ask, "What can we do to relieve it?"
We should not be so overwhelmed and discouraged
That we just throw up our hands and simply quit

What happened to the compassion of Job's friends?
When they got caught up in religiosity?
They had ears and eyes but were deaf and blind
They could not hear, nor could they see

We live in a world of human suffering
With multitudes with no food to eat
With many wrongfully imprisoned
With many impoverished who can not stand on their own two feet

While many live their lives in the comfort zone
For temporary worldly pleasures
Yet they seem never to be content or satisfied
They always seek ways to add to their worldly treasures

They give no thought to those around them
It is like they have blinders on their eyes
They seem oblivious and show no concern for others
Ignoring their pleas while turning a deaf ear to their cries

But some when they are stripped of their creature comforts
They tend more earnestly to seek God's face
It squeezes them in a corner so to speak
They come to cry out for God's mercy and His grace

Job spoke of the commonality of humanity
And the sovereignty of God
He pondered heart wrenching questions
He did not hide behind a superficial facade

Job expressed the deepest aspirations of the human heart
As he questioned his own suffering and agony
Reminding us that difficult questions lead to ultimate questions
Eventually he ends up asking about eternity

That the innocent suffer is plain to see
Just look at the little children in the womb
What is supposed to be a safe haven for the blameless
Has for multitudes become their tomb

How quickly things can turn around
There is no room for pride or self-confidence
Job did not suffer for any wrongdoing of his own
In his eyes his suffering made no sense

The book of Job is a literary masterpiece
The book of Job is a poetic drama
That speaks directly to human suffering
A wealth of insight into this human dilemma

In the beginning God created a paradise
For Adam and his wife
There was no anger or bitterness in the Garden
There was no disharmony, hostility or strife

Here we have a window into the ways of God in the world
Of a life wrenched by unexpected grief and turbulence
It helps give us a clear picture of the spiritual realm
And today this story needs to be heard for its relevance
Job 1:6

This story of high drama in the heavenlies
Helps us to interpret and understand
The painful and often haphazard experiences on this earth
And grasp what the Fall has done to this sin-cursed land

Job, though limited in his knowledge of God
Though not perfect chose to do what is right
Fearing God and turning from what is evil
Thus, he was a man who was blameless in God's sight
Job 1:8

Yes, Job was rich and a man of wisdom
But as we reflect maybe we can understand
Was not Solomon rich and full of wisdom?
Is there not some character flaw in every man?

With possessions that would be the envy of his friends
Yet he was a man of fairness and decency
He was a godly father to his children
He was an upright man with integrity
Job 1:3; Job 1:5

But his idyllic life was about to change
Soon he would be cloaked with a deep darkness one could feel
The spiritual forces of darkness would have their way
For what cannot be seen with the naked eye is very real
Job 1:13-19; Colossians 1:15-20

Everything he considered dear would be torn from him
The death of his ten children and his wealth
Even the strength of his own distraught wife would waver
And eventually he would even lose his health
Job 2:9

He is about to embark on a completely different life
That is directly opposite to what he had known
Much of the affliction would come in a single day
Causing his spirit inwardly to wail and groan

There was no one more impoverished than Job
Everything was taken away from him
And he sat down in dust and ashes
His sore covered body was gaunt and thin

Let us delve into this true and suspenseful story
Let us put this made-for-viewing drama before our eyes
By considering the three personalities involved in it
You might find yourself astonished and surprised
Ezekiel 14:14, 20; James 5:10-11

We have the personality of God
And we have the personality of Satan too
And we have the personality of all mankind
And let us not forget that includes both me and you

Right at the beginning we see Job and Satan
But the curtain opens with God at the center stage
After all, He is the prime mover behind the scenes
In this story of this ancient sage
Job 1:6

We see that God plays a role in our suffering
We see that Satan does not have complete control
Within the sovereignty of God our suffering is permitted
It is not as if God is ignorant or does not know

Poems Of Inspiration

If we were to look for the devil
It is a curious thing
We would not think to look for him in Heaven
Where the holy angel's dwell and sing

But that is exactly where we find him
For he is the enemy of our soul
And he brings slanderous accusations against us in the court of Heaven
This is a fact of which so many do not know
Revelation 12:10

God actually gives Satan permission
One may well ask, "How can this be?"
Within the plans and purposes of God
Does there not remain a mystery?
Deuteronomy 29:29

So, was Job's calamity from God or was it from the devil?
Ask yourself, whose desire was it to inflict the pain?
And then there is the Sabeans who attacked Job's servants
And remember Abel who was murdered by his brother Cain

The suffering originated within the plans and purposes of God
We see He is an active player in Job's plight
But when one experiences the affliction in the tunnel
They may lose hope they will ever again get a glimpse of light
Job 19:25

Do you think it unwise to speak so candidly?
About God's role in human suffering and pain
How often we take for granted the sunshine
How often we neglect to give thanks for the life-giving rain

You are the Salt of the Earth

Of course, we should never blame God for human suffering
For the word "blame" implies someone acted irresponsibly
But to say our suffering comes from God; that he permitted it
Is to simply affirm God's sovereignty

Often depicted as a contest between God and Satan
When in fact there is no contest at all
Defeated, Satan is quickly out of the overall picture
In the eyes of God, he is very small

But there was a contest between those who asked the questions
And those who tried to answer them
Questions that were debated during the time of Job
Questions that by many will be debated to the very end

The subject of Job is human suffering
In a world presumably made by God
Presumably by a God who himself does not suffer
Debated by those who in their own minds are at odds

Yet the Job's in this world continue to suffer
Clearly God had a different purpose in mind
Beyond winning a victory in a supposed "contest" with Satan
Reflect on Job's three friends and Jobs repine

Why do people put the blame on God?
For the evil things that people do
And if we are honest with ourselves
Is there not a touch of evil inside both me and you?
Romans 3:23

I can attest to this in my own life
I still have many struggles that take place within
Satan is always there to remind me of my failures
As I struggle with a lifetime battle with sin
Revelation 12:10

Poems Of Inspiration

Personally, all I can do is thank God for His mercy
Because I know the evil inside of me
And I can see the flaws and blemishes of others
For we all have eaten fruit from the forbidden tree
Matthew 7:11; Romans chapter 11; Genesis 2:16

Much of the pain and suffering I have experienced
Is due to my own lack of self-discipline
My lack of self-control over my sinful nature
That nature of sin that still dwells within
Romans Chapter seven

Mankind's freewill and the sovereignty of God
Is this too not a mystery?
Even Satan was given a freewill
And Adam and Eve choose to eat the forbidden fruit
from the tree
Isaiah 14:13-14 Genesis 3:6

Job could look at his calamity
As coming from God's almighty hand
But remember, God has given us a free will
And remember that there is evil in the land

It did not occur to Job to curse the wind
Nor did it occur to him to curse the Sabeans
Most important he did not curse the God of Heaven
Nor did he curse the Chaldeans

Listen to these words from the lips of Job
Shall I only accept God when He is good to me?
Job responded to the measure of his faith
At this point Job passed the test of his own soul admirably
Job 2:10

The Bible clearly teaches that God is the first cause
And yet He allows his creatures the freedom of choice
Even those who choose to embrace deception and wickedness
Closing their ears to His gracious voice
Ezekiel 18:23; 32

God is able to prevent or stop all the suffering
And if we take the time to look
That for the Christian all suffering will indeed come to an end
We find this in the final chapters of God's Book
Revelation 21:1

The wicked shall not escape God's righteous judgment
For the pride of sinners sets God against them
The fulfillment of Revelation is yet in the future
And their rebellion will indeed come to an end
Psalm 1; Matthew 25:41; Revelation chapter 20

Since the Fall of mankind in the Garden
There has been a curse upon the land
Sin has had devastating consequences on everything
Not just on the woman and the man
Romans 8:22-24

It is Satan who implements the suffering
But since the Fall man has had a bent toward sin
And not one of us can make the claim that we are sinless
All one need do is look within
Proverbs 20:9; John 9:41

Job was aware of his own sinfulness
And he was aware of his children's sinfulness too
And a good question each of us should ask ourselves
Is there not a sin nature inside both me and you?
Job 7:21; Job 1:5; Romans 3:23

Poems Of Inspiration

Children do not need to be taught how to be selfish
It comes naturally to them
A loving parent will instruct and teach a child
They will not castigate and condemn
Psalm 139:13-16

To be a Christian is to be a child of God
A Father who loves His children with a lavish love
And our heavenly Father wants us to draw near to Him
He wants us to set our hearts and minds on things above
1st John 3:1; James 4:8; Colossians 3:1-11

Satan too is a father with children
People become his children by their own free choice
It isn't just Jesus saying, "Come follow me"
We are free to ignore or listen to his voice
John 8:44-45; Proverbs 9:13-18; Matthew 4:19

Satan was a murderer from the beginning
He was man's tempter to that great sin
The sin that brought death into this world
How much the Pharisees were just like him
John 8:44

The Jews called the devil the angel of death
And was it not an unnatural thing
Was it not the devil himself that filled their hearts?
That their desire was to kill the King of kings

Is God blind to human suffering?
Listen to what Job had to say
"Blessed be the name of the LORD"
"The LORD gave, and the LORD has taken away"
Proverbs 15:3; Job 1:21-23

You are the Salt of the Earth

Heaven awaits the child of God
Today we know so much more than Job knew way back then
For we have the New Covenant in Jesus
This Holy One who came to cleanse us of our sin

It was the marauders that did the pillaging
And the disastrous whether that caused the calamity
But Job could see beyond the evil that had befallen him
He had a grasp of God's power and sovereignty

Every kingdom has a king
Some are good, and some are bad
God established the family as a unit for a purpose
Every child should have a mother and a dad

But darkness has entered this sin cursed world
And divorce has become common place
But God offers forgiveness to those in darkness
He extends to all His mercy and His grace

As I reflect on all the pain both physical and emotional
That I have experienced in my life
And upon my parents and my siblings
And upon my children and my wife

My grandparents died many years ago
My mother died when I was only one
My father and both of my sisters and my brother has
died as well
I am my parent's only remaining son

I see that certain situations that we face in life
Weigh heavily on our soul
Tempting to drain us of our spiritual vitality
Yet cannot such seasons in life help us to mature and grow?
Romans 5:3; James 1:2-4

Many understand the pain of physical suffering
But there is another suffering that takes it toll
Wanting to drown us in the dark waters of despair
Suffering that is mental, spiritual and emotional

Pain forces us to look beyond our immediate circumstances
It has a way of getting our attention
It makes us look at life in a different way
We cannot ignore the stress brought on by the tension

Suffering drives us to ask the big questions
It makes us look at reality in the face
"Why am I here" and "What's the purpose of my life?"
Suffering can make us focus on God's amazing grace

I seen a sticker on the back window of a car
That read, "Some disabilities can't be seen"
Imagine the crippling emotions of a child
Abused by a bully who is cruel and mean

Have you gone through severe trials and testing?
It seems as if a dagger has been thrust into your heart
You have cried out, but the heavens have remained silent
Your world seems to be falling apart

Have you experienced the abuse of a spouse?
Brought on by a growing disrespect
Or possibly by a roaming eye and marital unfaithfulness
Or simply brought on by neglect

Some people never give God a second thought
They never take the time to ask or knock or seek
They think it is foolish to believe in an unseen God
And look down on those who do as being weak

Matthew 7:7

Such people put themselves in place of God
The Bible says that those who do so are a fool
God's Majestic Creation leaves men without excuse
For His Creation declares His glory to me and you
Psalm 14:1; Romans 1:20; Psalm 19

It is often in the season of trial and suffering
That God gets our attention and opens our eyes
For the conditions are right for us to grow in spiritual maturity
It is then that God's purposes are often realized

Cannot our lives be described as a journey?
A journey with many challenges along the way
A journey with seasons of joy and sunshine
And seasons when the skies are dark and grey

We cannot see the entire road that stretches ahead of us
We do not know what the future has in store
We can make our plans and have our dreams
But we do not know what awaits us on the other side of the door
James 4:14

Of course, the door of which I speak
Only deals with the uncertainties in this life
Because we know that heaven awaits the Christian in the future
Those who have repented and placed their faith in Jesus Christ
John 10:28-30

In writing this poem I feel so inadequate
Sometimes I complain about the littlest thing
How often my lips move because of rote memory
But my heart is not in the songs I sing

Job's suffering is described in graphic terms
One would almost think he was in Hell
Boils, ulcers, and other painful skin diseases
And his putrid breath that had an awful smell

He was subject to sleeplessness and depression
His suffering was consuming and intense
Even his friends became his accusers
Instead of coming to his defense

He was a portrait of disfigurement
I cannot imagine the anguish of his soul
Even the children ridiculed and scorned him
He was a loner with no one to console

Satan had predicted Job would curse God to his face
At the loss of his wealth and family
And the physical diseases that were inflicted upon him
That caused so much pain and agony

But what was going on in Job's emotions?
What thoughts and feelings were surging in his mind?
When the evidence mounted that God had turned against him
What will we discover what will we find?

When Job could no longer hold in his anguish
Verbally it spills out in a flood of despair
Wishing he could be blotted out from history
As if it were his earnest prayer

Through the most severe trials we see Job's integrity
We get a glimpse into Job's heart
We see in his relationship with God his motives were pure
We see this on the onset of the trials when they start

What about those of us in church today?
Would we bless God if poverty instantly replaced our wealth?
Would we accuse God if death has stolen away our children?
Would we curse God if we lost our health?

II Corinthians 1:9

Or would we fall to the ground and worship God?
And affirm His right to give and take away?
Even though our grief would be overwhelming
This is the question put before us today
Job 1:21

Job did not have the complete revelation of God
When the severe trials and tempests came his way
But we as Christians have the Bible in its entirety
That we hold in our hands today

The question that is put before each one of us
Is, "Do we only serve God because it is profitable?"
Do we really understand the love of the God of Calvary?
Do we know Him as the lover of our soul?

I personally came to God because of dreadful fear
Because I was reaping the consequences of what I had sown
I came to understand my wretchedness before a Holy God
That I had no merit or righteousness to stand before
Him on my own

This dark dreadful fear had befallen me
Because of the lifestyle I had chosen had taken its toll
Unlike the sufferings Job
I brought the sufferings upon my own soul

And I am still reaping some of the consequences to this very day
My imbalance is at times quite intense
Nightmares and hallucinations as I sleep
At times overwhelming and immense

Has God got your full attention?
As a result of your suffering and pain
Will you draw near to him and cry out mercy!
Or will you curse His Holy name?

Ah, "The Gospel according to Matthew"
The second part of the Bible is entitled the new covenant
Because it is about the work and person of Jesus Christ
Thus, we have what is called "The New Testament"

All the grace we need is found in Jesus
Yet, unless we consent to him as our Lord
We cannot expect any benefit by him as Savior
We need to be interwoven with him like a fastening cord

With what pleasure do we read
The last will and testament of a friend?
How great is the love the Father has lavished upon us
If we could only grasp and comprehend
John 15:15; 1st John 3:1

To make this New Testament effectual
It was necessary that Christ should die
If asked, "Why do you identify yourself as a Christian?"
The answer, "The cross is the reason why."

To distinguish it from that which was given to Moses
The covenant of Christ is called the New Testament
Repeatedly foretold and proclaimed by the prophets of the old
Of this Holy One that would be sent
Luke 24:27

Emmanuel, God is with us
Jesus was and is fully God and fully man
Mary's miraculous conception fulfilled Isaiah's prophecy
A mystery we may not fully grasp or understand
Isaiah 7:14; John 1:1, 14; Matthew 1:22-23

The enemy of God is the devil
In his first state the object of God's love
Before he perverted his position of authority
Determined to dethrone the God seated high above

In the Middle Ages imaginative portrayals of Satan abounded
Even today some see him as Hell's proprietor
As if he had the exclusive title to it
As if he was its owner and possessor

The Bible presents Satan as a powerful being
As one who is an active enemy of God
At times appearing as an angel of light
Well disguised behind a superficial façade

Once known as the "bright star" of the morning
Apart from the Holy Trinity he was the highest being
Ezekiel says, "You were the anointed Cherub"
Clarifying that he was not a human king
Ezekiel 28:14

Heaven is a court because God is the center of order
The center of whom all things turn
The Scriptures do reveal the answers to life's questions For
all who have a desire and willingness to learn

Satan wants to bring out the worst in us
God wants to bring out our best
Satan tempts us to do evil
God wants to refine us through each trial and each test

How you have fallen from heaven
Because of your arrogance and pride
And you will not stand in the Day of Judgment
A judgment from which you cannot escape or hide
Isaiah 14:12; Revelation 20:11-15

Nor will those who reject the living Christ
This One sent from the Father above
This One who willingly died to take our place
To demonstrate the Father's love

Before the fall of Satan
He was colorful and beautiful
Living in the very presence of God
He was gifted and musical

But he defiled his sanctuaries
In pride his "heart was lifted up"
He was the anointed cherub before his rebellion
Before self-sufficiency filled his cup
Ezekiel 28:17

Satan's free will is seen in his five "I will" statements
They reveal Satan's self-sufficiency
His arrogance is the opposite of love and obedience
His pride is the opposite of meekness and humility

Satan is not a red demon with a pitchfork in his hand
He is not a fictitious imaginary being
Wars, divorce, abuse, death and diseases
His influence in this world is clearly seen

An authentic minister wears no mask
But Satan masquerades as an angel of light
He calls evil good and what is good he calls evil
Should we not reflect on what influenced Eve and that first bite?
II Corinthians 11:14; Isaiah 5:20; Genesis 2:16-17

Satan does not haunt us with his ugliness
He does not smell of brimstone but cologne
A charming figure who later tempted Jesus in the wilderness
Wanting Jesus to bow down to him and him alone
Matthew 4:9

Satan does not inquire for the purpose of honest investigation
That is not his desire or his aim
His purpose is to prosecute regardless of the means
He is Adversary, and his objective is to simply cast the blame
1st Peter 5:8

He is like a chameleon that changes color
He is a master of disguise
Successfully concealing his true identity
Thus, Jesus called him the "father of lies"
John 8:44

Sometimes he puts on the garb of generals
Sometimes he is friendly and polite
As Christians we need to have discernment
For Satan masquerades as an angel of light
II Corinthians 11:14

With no regard to honor, right or justice
Satan is the corruptor of all that is good
He manipulates the weak willed and the vulnerable
While all the time whimpering "I'm so misunderstood"

Satan is persistent and determined
He is the author of confusion
He is the master at creating disharmony
He has great skill in creating an illusion

Metaphors of resurrection are all around us
We see it in new generations and in every spring
When new flowers burst forth on the hillside
When the birds of the air return to sing

When we are full of joy and satisfaction
Often when all is going well
We may lose our eternal perspective
That there are those who are on their way to eternal Hell

We may start to wallow in our comfort
And forget to set our hearts and minds on things above
We may forget our purpose for why we are here
To point others to the cross and Jesus' love
Colossians 3:1-4; Matthew 28:16-20

Joy and grief at the same time
How could that be possible?
A bittersweet experience for a Christian
When we see a loved one go

We give Bibles to our children
But read little of it ourselves
Jesus said, "Man does not live on bread alone"
How often our Bibles sit unused on dusty shelves
Matthew 4:4

There are those who scream and shout from behind the pulpit
And there are Bible thumpers in the home
And there are those who only speak of love
Those who speak of love and love alone

In many churches today
Biblical love has been replaced with sentimentalism
And intellect has been replaced as well
With anti-intellectualism

Often truth is smothered by our feelings and emotions
Emotions blur the vision of our eyes
Satan will use whatever method to deceive us
To entrap us with his deadly lies

Things have come to a sorry pass
When God's Word begins to interfere with our private life
But God knows the secrets of the heart
Of every husband and every wife

Jesus shed drops of blood in the Garden
For the cleansing of our sins there was a price to pay
But let us not forget the victorious resurrection
You see death does not have the final say
Luke 22:44; Romans 6:23; John 11:25

How often we read the obituaries
And fail to grasp what has taken place
That there awaits a judgment for unrepentant sinners
Those who have scorned and mocked at God's amazing grace
Matthew 25:41; Matthew 27:30

And that the Christian too is accountable
For the talents placed in his care
In the parables Jesus gave us serious awakening warnings
To quicken us with the upmost care
Matthew 13:34

That we might be diligent until his second coming
And put our talents to good use
But will we be as those who try to justify their negligence?
And stand before Him with a faulty excuse
Matthew 25:24-25

Or will we be as those who have the blessed assurance?
Can we with Job make this declaration?
I know that my Redeemer lives!
Can we confidently make this proclamation?
Job 19:25

And that we will stand again at the later day
And though our body is destroyed it too will rise
And we too will see the God of Heaven in all His glory
We ourselves with our own eyes
Job 19:25-27

Job's friends and the Pharisees
And the planks embedded in my own eyes
How often we are fault-finding and nitpicking
And the God of Heaven we trivialize
Matthew 7:3-5

How often we attend Good Friday services
Simply out of custom and tradition
Like little children content with their chocolate bunnies
Without real reflection and conviction

Today many churches are divorced from the God of Heaven
Some void of love some void of truth
The sins of the fathers have been passed down to their children
Leaving behind bewildered and disconnected youth

With ears that are dull of hearing
How often we gather, and we perch
How often do we merely listen?
Yet make no effort to ask and seek and search
James 1:22-25; Matthew 7:7

Listen closely to the life of Jesus
Saying if a man would follow me
Let him know and declare his purpose
Let him acknowledge his mortality

Jesus knew the value of a soul
And this should steal away our breath
For the redemption of a soul
Would be at the price of his own death

As I write at this very moment
My feelings long to take control
Because I am experiencing a strong chemical imbalance
A spiritual darkness wants to smother my soul

I know that there is a God up in the Heavens
But right now, He seems so impersonal
And yet as I sit here, I lift my prayers to Him
What is the alternative were else can I go?
Matthew 7:7; John 6:68

If the foundation of my faith is in my feelings
Then I would be damned and eternally lost
But God's existence is overwhelming
And so is the reality of the cross
Psalm 19; Romans 1:20

I do not have enough faith to be an atheist
I cannot help but believe in this God I cannot see
I can relate to the words penned by the palmist
Who am I that you are mindful of me?
Psalm 8

When we come to know God as a loving sovereign God
The God who is standing over all human history
And that he is weaving it all together
In a stunning and beautiful tapestry

And that He has prepared a place for those who love Him
Where all our tears will be wiped away
Then it will give us the strength to persevere
As we anticipate that glorious day
John 14:3; Revelation 21:4

Not all will be singing the songs as Job did
On this side of heaven's glory
They may endure suffering to the very end
Ongoing pain may fill their earthly story

Like those who climb high mountains
With a goal to reach the top
At times, the climb can be hard going
When the voices in your head are telling you to stop

Though the trail seems to stretch endlessly before you
And you realize that the journey is not a piece of cake
You are always getting nearer to your destination
With each and every step you take

Every day brings you one step closer
Then the previous day before
Your entrance to heaven will soon be a reality
Where your tears will cease to be for evermore

And just like it was for Jesus' journey
There is a joy set before you and me
So, let us endure with patience the hardship of the trail
That will lead us into a glorious eternity

Written for God's glory

19. We too will Rise!

Trees in the winter season appear to be lifeless
They appear that way for a good reason
With no foliage to adorn them as in the summer
Naked and bare during the winter season

Christian, do not doubt God's promises
Do not listen to the devil's lies
Remember spring always follows winter
And like our Savior we too will rise
Hebrews 6:18; Titus 1:2; John 8:44; John 11:25, 26

Like the trees of the winter season
Those anticipating the coming spring
With the promise of buds mysteriously and miraculously appearing
Followed by the luscious foliage that they will bring
Psalm 1

We have this promise from our Savior
This promise from our all-loving God
Of a glorious, resurrected body
That with great power it will break through the earthly sod
1st Corinthians 15:42-58

Examples of death followed by resurrection blossom
all around us
God has placed them before us plain and clear
Dormant seeds die in order to bring forth a harvest
We see resurrection each spring of the year
John 12:24; Hosea 6:3

It is certain that seeds undergo a great change
By a mysterious wonderful power
A transformation takes place as the seed bursts forth
from the earth
No longer a seed but a beautiful fragrant flower
Romans 12:1-2; Mark 4:26-29; II Corinthians 2:15

Flowers with a sweet-smelling aroma
With many exotic colors and varieties
Butterflies sipping their sweet nectar
Flowers providing food for the honeybees
Ephesians 5:1-2; Proverbs 27:9; Colossians 3:11; Psalm 19:10

When we lay a loved one's empty vessel to rest
It is like committing a seed to the earth
We have God's promise of its glorious resurrection
Free from death and decay and sin's dreadful curse
II Corinthians 5:1

To be reunited with our spirit
For the spirit never dies
Having entered into the very presence of God
Like on the wings of eagles that effortlessly rise
John 11:25-26; II Corinthians 5:8

God has placed imitations of immortality around us
He has placed them everywhere
Look at the beautiful butterfly
As it soars effortlessly in the air

William Jennings Bryan, in a sense
Has giving us an excellent paraphrase
To the pondering of Job's heart
To the question that Job raised
Job 14:14

If our loving Heavenly Father
Deigns to touch with divine power
The cold and pulseless heart of a buried seed
And bring forth from the earth a graceful flower
Genesis 1:12

Or make an acorn buried in the earth
Burst forth from its prison wall
To rise high above the earth
To grow up strong and tall

Will He leave neglected
In the earth the soul of man
Made the image of his Creator
Would such a thing fit into His plan?

If He stoops down to give a rosebush
Those whose withered blossoms float upon the autumn breeze
The sweet assurance of another spring
If He would do this for one of these

Or consider the tiny seed of a giant Redwood
That is planted in the earth
That when it dies unto itself
A mighty tree is given birth

And look at the amazing chrysalis
And the beautiful monarch butterfly
Before the butterfly came into existence
A caterpillar had to die

No longer an earthbound caterpillar
No longer a lowly earthbound worm
But a creature of exquisite beauty
Is there not a lesson we should learn?

So once the frost of winter comes
To the sons of men
Will He refuse them the hope of His promise?
That they too will rise again

No, for we have this blessed hope
We need not believe the devil's lies
Like Christ, the firstborn from the dead
We too like Him will rise
Colossians 1:18

Fear not that your life shall come to an end
But rather that it shall never have a beginning
Said Cardinal Newman, speaking of our need of Jesus Christ
A life transformed by grace— —a life worth living
John 3:1-16

Christians will be ushered into His presence
When we leave this life behind
We who put our trust and hope in Jesus
Like the stars we too will shine
Luke 16:22; Philippians 2:15

There is a future rest for the people of God
A rest from death, sorrow and sin
The future rest will abundantly recompense all these present sufferings
Both those from without and from within

Today multitudes are rebelling against the light of nature
And against the light of divine revelation as well
One day the righteous will enter God's glorious
eternal Kingdom
While the wicked will be cast into the flames of eternal Hell
Psalm 1; Matthew 25:41

A Brief Prayer

I thank you great God of Heaven
The Author and Sustainer of life
For the promises we find in Scriptures
That we find in Jesus Christ
Hebrews 1:3; II Corinthians 1:19

Confirm in our mind the hope
That we have eternal life after death
Through Jesus Christ our Lord and Savior
Once we breathed our final breath
Luke 23:43

Eternal Father, thank you for the unspeakable joys
You have prepared for others and me
That the end of time leads us into your presence
Secure for all eternity
1st Corinthians 2:9

Written for the glory of God
Inspired by others and God's precious Word

Please take the time to look up the Scripture verses referenced
in this poem for the Scriptures themselves are God's Word!

20. What won't be in Heaven

There won't be any hospitals in heaven
There will be no tears to cloud our eyes
There won't be any broken homes or broken hearts
There won't be any deception – no more lies

There won't be any emptiness or sadness
There won't be any more crying – no more tears
There won't be any more terrorist or bombings
There won't be any more anxiousness or fears

There won't be any loneliness in heaven
There won't be any more hunger, no poverty
There won't be any sickness or blindness
For all will clearly see

There won't be a doctor's office in heaven
There won't be any hospital waiting rooms
There won't be a single grave site
There will be no more depression, no more gloom

Not a single impure thought will be in heaven
Not one impure thought will enter heaven's door
There will be no harsh words spoken in heaven
They will cease to be forevermore

You are the Salt of the Earth

There will be no painful comparisons in heaven
There will be no sibling rivalry
There will be no favoritism or favorites
There will be no disharmony

There will be no isolation in heaven
There will be no more emotional or mental pain
There will be no hopelessness in heaven
There will be no more stress or no more strain

There will be no separation in heaven
From friends or family
There will be no more dividing walls or prisons
For all who enter will be free

There will be no fabrication in heaven
There will be no falsehood or dishonesty
There will be no unfaithfulness or cunning
There will be no hypocrisy

There will be no divorce in heaven
There will be no orphan without a home
There will be no desertion or withdrawal
There will be no one abandoned or left alone

There will be no child abuse in heaven
There will be no exploitation of our youth
There will be no more phoniness or fallacies
There will be no distortion of the truth

There will be no wheelchairs up in heaven
And there will be no paralysis
There will be no weaknesses or frailties
There will be no more tumors, no more cysts

There will be no temptations up in heaven
From without or from within
For all those who put their trust in Jesus
For those who have been "born again"

There will be no more diseases up in heaven
Of the body or the mind
There will be no more painful memories
For they will all be left behind

None of these things will be found in heaven
And many more things could be added to the list
If we did an exposition or a treatise
If we did an orderly systematic analysis

Inspired by Anne Graham Lotz
From her book- "Heaven My Father's House"

I wrote this while Sue, my wife, was in the hospital sometime in December of 2003.

While hanging on the cross, the thief came to understand his sin in a short period of time and asked Jesus, "remember me when you come into your kingdom." Jesus responded, "today you will be with me in paradise". It is not too late to acknowledge your sins and ask Jesus to forgive you.

21. God's Questions

Where were you when I laid the earths foundation?
Tell me if you can
You who dare to darken my counsel
Brace yourself like a man

Who marked off its dimensions?
Surely you know! ……you are so wise!
Who stretched a measuring line across it?
Who set in place the skies?

On what were its footings set?
Or who laid its cornerstone?
While the morning stars all sang together
Who gave the earth its home?

Who shut the sea behind closed doors?
When it burst forth from the womb
When I made the clouds its garment
Contained to its own room

When I wrapped it in thick darkness
And set in place its bars and doors
When I said, this far you may come and no further
When I gave boundaries to its shores

Poems Of Inspiration

Have you ever given orders to the morning?
Or shown the dawn its locality
Where the wicked are denied their light
Where they no longer cease to be

Have you journeyed through the springs?
Or the vastness of the sea
Or walked in the recesses of the deep
Are you the one that holds the key?

Have the gates of death been shown to you?
Are they not hidden from your sight?
Have you seen the gates of the deep shadows?
Are they not to you like the blackest night?

And the vast expanses of the earth
Have you comprehended these?
Tell me if you know all this
Tell me would you please

What is the way to the abode of light?
And where does the darkness hide?
Can you take me to their places?
Do you know where they reside?

Do you know the paths to their dwelling?
Have you entered into the storehouses of the snow?
You have lived so many years
These things you surely know

Have you seen the storehouses of the hail?
Which I reserve for times of trouble
For days of war and battle
To turn strong walls into rubble

What is the way to their place?
Where the lightning is dispersed
Or the place where the east winds are scattered
Over all the earth

Who cuts a channel for the torrents of rain?
A path for the thunderstorm
To water a land where no man lives
To water a desolate wasteland once forlorn

Does the rain have a father?
Who fathers the drops of dew?
Who unleashes the lightning?
It surely is not you

From whose womb comes the ice?
Who gives birth to the frost and snow?
Who brings waters down from heaven?
Who causes the grass to grow?

Can you bind the beautiful Pleiades?
Can you loose the cords of Orion?
Can you bring forth the constellations in their seasons?
Can you number the stars one by one?

Can you lead out the Bear with its cubs?
The laws of heavens do you understand
Can you set up God's dominion over the earth?
Are you not just a man?

Written for the Glory of God
Inspired from the Book of Job
Finished on October 29th, 2007

GENESIS 1:1 In the beginning God created the heaven and the earth.

ISAIAH 40:22 It is he that sitteth upon the circle of the earth, and the inhabitants thereof are as grasshoppers: that stretches out the heavens as a curtain, and spreadeth them out as a tent to live in.

PSALM 8:3, 4 When I consider thy heavens, the work of thy fingers, the moon and the stars, which thou hast ordained; What is man, that thou art mindful of him? and the son of man, that thou visitest him?

Deuteronomy 29:29 The secret things belong unto the Lord our God: but those things which are revealed belong unto us and our children for ever that we may do all the words of this law.

Job Chapter 38

Part Two.

...Confronting the sin of our silence!

LETTERS TO THE EDITOR

1. Bruised Reeds and Smoldering Wicks

My, how time flies. Christmas and New Years are now past. A couple of weeks ago our associate pastor showed our congregation a T-shirt with the saying "I thought growing old would take longer" written on it. We laughed because many of us could relate to the saying. Billy Graham, the renowned evangelist once said, "I was prepared for dying but I was never prepared for growing old". Following our laughter our Pastor's message was convicting and was met to tug on our heartstrings concerning our relationship with Christ.

Recently I watched a program remembering the many Hollywood actors that died this past year leaving their loved ones to grieve. Some were young and some were old. Being young is no guarantee of a long life. Aging should put things in perspective and make us think about and prepare for the inevitable.

These deaths and as seen from these articles in last years BCR newspaper we can see that last year was not happy for many nor was their Christmas merry... Child Abuse Awareness Month Comes to a Close...Cyber bullying in our schools...Heroin hits home...Drugs, depression, suicide—-and more...Sex offenders, schools and safety...And many personal stories could be added to this list.

And yes, there were many uplifting and encouraging and humorous articles too, stories of people giving back to the community through their service and financial support, the joy of new births, stories of wedding plans, humorous stories by Greg Wallace, and stories of those who by God's grace have overcome huge obstacles in their lives.

Looking at the upcoming New Year realistically we will see that in many ways it will be much the same as the year we are leaving behind. There will be joys and sadness, victories and setbacks, weddings and divorces, people giving back to the community, new births and deaths. Sadly, the New Year will find many, who for the first time, will join with and fall under the category of being a bruised reed or smoldering wick as a result of some tragedy invading their lives.

Over 681 years before Jesus' birth, the prophet Isaiah said of him, "A bruised reed he will not break, and a smoldering wick he will not snuff out (Isaiah 42:3). We are living in a world where the results of sin are clearly seen, death being the ultimate one. Our sin affects others and other's sin affects us. In that sense we are all bruised reeds to some degree. Let us listen to what else Isaiah said about Jesus. "But He was wounded for our transgressions; He was _bruised_ for our iniquities; and with His stripes we are healed" (Isaiah 53:5).

Let us no longer hide our faces from Jesus but let us esteem him. (Isaiah 53, the whole chapter). For we, like many others, may not be here to usher in another New Year (James 4:13-17). So why not join in today with those who are reaching out to others.

2. Are you in a Hurry?

If you are in an Olympic race being fast and winning is important. But a Christian's life is a race of perseverance and it should be our goal to bring others across the finish line with us. What about our spiritual race? Think of "The Tortoise and the Hare." One of the metaphors used in the Scriptures about our Christian "walk" is that our spiritual journey is a race. 1st Corinthians 9:24-27.

Shamefully, I myself have run for most of it instead of walked. Plus, I had the distorted goal of memorizing the entire New Testament. My mind got to a place (a dark place) where it was racing so fast, I was unable to read anything and retain it. I could rattle off passages of Scripture but was "at times" far from applying the principles they contained.

My wife's deep-rooted faith and patience and love and perseverance helped me through those turbulent times. How much like Christ she has been through the years! I am not ashamed of being bi-polar but for the pride that has accompanied it at times, standing on my pedestal and thinking, "I know and can quote so much Scripture!" Jesus said, "Come, follow me" but I was so busy doing his Kingdom work that I neglected the King. I went through a cycle of extreme running followed by extreme fatigue, faith followed by doubt, joy followed by guilt, accomplishments followed be defeat, feeling secure followed by insecurities, from having courage to becoming fearful, from being patient to being impatient (think rollercoaster) all the while telling the Lord to hurry up and catch up to me. Imagine my arrogance of telling the Lord what to do!

Saying I was out of balance is an understatement! Read Ecclesiastes 7:16-18. Pride is an ugly thing. I did not balance memorizing Scripture with prayerful study, meditation, reading, or listening to God's word.

Our feelings, good works or how much we do will not eradicate our sins. If our Salvation depended on any of these there would be no hope for any of us. "For it is by grace you have been saved through faith...a gift from God". Jesus said, "It is finished". Focus on the word "finished" as it has to do with God's work. Salvation on our behalf was provided for us on the cross. It is called grace. Think of the acrostic G.R.A.C.E.

G-od's

R-iches

A-t

C-hrist's

E-xpense

To think we can earn God's love is insulting to him! "We love him because he first loved us" (1st John 4:19). Our good works will follow as we build on the foundation of his grace. There is huge difference between arrogance and humility, between struggling with sin and embracing sin. Coming out of an abusive painful childhood or a deeply rooted sinful lifestyle allows "time" for God's grace to bring healing and do its work and sadly it also gives the enemy of our soul "time" to tempt, accuse and bring accusations. Both take place in a Christian's life. Are you in a hurry? May I suggest you slow down? You may, like me, find that you can accomplish more by doing less. Balance is the key.

3. Questions to Ponder

Yoo-hoo. Is there anybody out there? Today we live in a world influenced by highspeed advancing technology while at the same time in a society infatuated with science fiction, fantasy and people embracing philosophies parallel to that of fairy tales.

In 1974 the SETI program started its search for extraterrestrial intelligence. In their search of the great unknown, they theorized that there could be thousands of worlds like ours out there yet not even a single one has been found. NASA's total inflated adjusted costs have been more than $900 billion dollars since its creation in 1958. With all their worldly intelligence and technological achievements and extravagant spending is man really all that wise?

Let us do a little research of our own and ask a few soul-searching questions. If there are civilizations like ours out there would they, like us, murder their innocent children by means of abortion? Would their siblings be like Cain and Able with one brother, who out of jealousy killed his innocent brother? Would two World Wars be in their past history? Would their entire history, like ours, be spotted with over 14,000 wars? Would they be on the same course as ours heading toward a predicted apocalypse? Would their nations strive to have nuclear warheads in preparation for such an apocalypse? Would their schools indoctrinate their children with the deadly philosophy of evolution and say that we are here as a result of an accident? Would they have overcrowded prisons? Would divorce and broken families and homeless people be a blemish on their land? Would the entertainment they embraced become more and more ungodly? Would murder be rampant in their big cities? Would they search for life on other planets, and if so, why, what would they be looking for? Would they put locks on their doors? Would multitudes grow weary of doing good and become discouraged and withdraw from the battle of doing right and no longer fight for their children? Would there be many manmade religions so they could do as they please as a result of rejecting the Creator who reveals Himself in Scripture? Would there be nearly 7,665, 000 people die of starvation each year and nearly a billion go to bed hungry every night? Would they turn a deaf ear to the teachings of Jesus and justify their own sins?

"Where is the wise man? Where is the scholar? Where is the philosopher of this age? Has not God made foolish the wisdom of the world? For since in the wisdom of God the world through its wisdom did not know Him, God was pleased through the foolishness of what was preached to save those who believe." (I Corinthians 1:20-21).

Our world is not in more need of more worldly knowledge and technology but of changed hearts. It is in need of God's mercy and grace, of godly wisdom. It is in need of being saved. It is in need of the Gospel of Jesus Christ.

4. A Message of Hope

Hope. Don't we all need hope? Not an imaginary hope built on wishful thinking (Matthew 7:24-29), our feelings, how good we are or on how much we do. But a real hope built on the foundation of truth. Luke 8:18. "Therefore consider carefully how you listen. Whoever has will be given more; whoever does not have, even what he thinks he has will be taken from him." Study note, *"consider carefully how you listen.* The disciples heard not only for themselves but also for those to whom they would minister (see Mark 4:24; James 1:19-22). Truth that is not appropriated will be lost (19:26), but truth that is used will be multiplied." (Matthew Henry).

Where can hope be found? Can government give us that kind of hope? No. There are many different forms of government and we see within our own much divisiveness. And yet, by God's grace, we have the best constitution in the world that many others have tried to emulate. Does science give us that kind of hope? No. Much of today's science is used for the development and the destruction of mankind. Does education give us that kind of hope? No. Remember our regression from being number one down to 17th in recent years. Does longevity of life give us that kind of hope? No. The older we get, unless we are living in denial, the more aware we are of our own mortality. Look at all the people who in their search of finding hope in staying young are exploited by a market ready to offer them the promise of the "Fountain of

Youth" and stop the relentless process of aging! Well, surely the answer can be found in religion. No, too many to choose from. How about wealth? No, you can't take it with you. Does the lottery offer that kind of hope? What are the "odds" of that? Does entertainment give us that kind of hope? No, godly entertainment is a way to relax and enjoy some of the good gifts that God has given us if done moderately, a place to go and get away from all of the stress and strain we experience in this life. No, entertainment isn't where real hope can be found, although it does help bring balance to our lives.

I believe that real hope built on a foundation of truth will affect how we feel, how good we will become, and how much we do and the motive for why we do what we do. Real hope based on truth will give real purpose to life.

If you are looking for purpose beyond the temporary things in this life, God's Word, the Bible, offers you that kind of hope through the work and person of Jesus Christ. Hebrews 6:19, 20. "We have this hope as an anchor for the soul, firm and secure. It enters the sanctuary behind the curtain, where Jesus, who went before us, has entered on our behalf."

5. A Religious World

Congress shall make no law respecting the establishment of religion...Today we live in a very "religious" world... Islam, Christianity, Atheism, Evolutionism, Judaism, Buddhism, Hinduism, Catholicism, Protestantism and many other ism's creating skepticism and confusion. "There is a way that seems right to a man but in the end it leads to death" (Proverbs 12:12). That should open our eyes! To be a Christian is to be a Christ follower. Pluralism in religions is an oxymoron. Each religion makes distinct truth claims. Read the seven "I am" claims of Jesus in the Gospel of John (see 6:35; 8:12; 9:5; 10:7,9;10:11, 14; 11:25; 14:6; 15:1,5).

Religions are based on a belief. 75% of Americans identify with a Christian religion. What does it mean to have faith? Is there such a thing as blind faith? Can one have a faith based on facts? What is a world view? What is a theory? What is truth? What does it mean to be deceptive or to be deceived? Can a person believe in Christ and not be saved and can one be willingly ignorant (the answer is yes)?

"Ignorance is bliss", or so the saying goes. One should ask, is it true that ignorance is bliss? Remember, there is a way that seems right...that leads to death.

The saying "What you don't know cannot hurt you" figures in a passage from "On a Distance Prospect of Eton College," by the eighteenth century English poet Thomas Gray: "Where ignorance is bliss, / 'Tis folly to be wise."

Recently my 11 year old granddaughter said, "I don't want to be hated." You see, we live in a world that has a lot of hateful people in it. Think of the movie "Mean Girls". The Bible says Christians are "to hate what is evil", not the evil doer's but the evil things they do and the evil within ourselves and the bent we have toward it. It costs something to follow Christ. God hates sin. Jesus, speaking of Christ followers, said, "If the world hates you, keep in mind that it hated me first, if you belonged to the world it would love you as its own. But you do not belong to the world, for I have chosen you out the world. That is why the world hates you."(John 15:19). People kill other people out of jealousy…hatred…by accident…because of greed…and in the name of religion. Jesus was killed by religious people because He told the truth and exposed their sin and hypocrisy. I use to mock those who identified with Christ. It's humbling to acknowledge one's sin. You see, when someone stands up for the truth there will be those who will hate you. Some might even seek to kill you.

Many believe being religious places them in a "safe place". But confessing Jesus Christ with our mouth and believing in our heart that God raised him from the dead and taking up our cross to follow Him might be costly.

6. I used to be a Fool!

I thought I was on a cruise ship to Paradise but found that I was on a ship of fools. What does fool safe mean? I used to be slow to listen and quick to speak. I used to be a thief, I really was, and I would steal things. I used to be a liar and at times purposefully twist the truth. I used to be ignorant of the things of God. I used to be filled with hatred toward some people. I used to be addicted to pornography. I used to be addicted to smoking cigarettes. I used to be an alcoholic. I used to be oppressed and treated unfairly in the workplace. I used to get bored at times. I used to be proficient in the use of vulgar language, and do not let anyone fool you, I wasn't speaking French (Pardon my French) and if I bump my head real hard a little French may come to the surface of my lips even today, some call it colorful language, but I believe it would fall under what the Bible describes as "filthy language" or "course joking". I used to put too much emphasis on my feelings instead of my faith based on facts and overwhelming evidence. I used to have chronic fatigue. I used to be filled with self pity. I used to be impatient. I used to and still do at times struggle with self-control. I used to have straying eyes and in the culture we live in today it is not easy to keep them from straying at times even now. I used to be narcissistic, yet I did not love myself. Is that even possible? Yes, one can love themselves in an unhealthy way, a destructive way. I used to be manic-depressed, bi-polar, out of balance (go figure).

By now it should be clear that I had eye ("I") problems. But with the help of a very patient and loving wife, a friend who sticks closer than a brother, a loving church body, a couple of therapists, medication, godly counsel, the Scriptures, and because of the Lord's great love and compassion (Jeremiah 3:20) and because "He who started a good work in me is faithful to bring it to completion until the day of Christ Jesus" (Philippians 1:6) I was not and am not consumed.

Proverbs 19:3 says: "A man's own folly ruins his life, yet his heart rages against the Lord." Folly comes from the Old French word meaning "madness, stupidity." When one embraces a life of folly one could rightly be called a fool. So yes, I used to be a fool. The Bible puts it this way, "For you were once darkness but now you are light in the Lord, live as children of light. Have nothing to do with the fruitless deeds of darkness but rather expose them."

Now I am reconciled, adopted into God's family, a friend of Jesus, a light, be it ever so small, in this dark world, I have always been loved by God but now I love Him, no longer foolish but growing in wisdom and building on a solid foundation (Matthew 7:24-29).

7. Did God Really Say?

Temptation comes in the form of a conversation hidden inside the secrecy of our own mind. The conversation comes in the form of subtle questions pregnant with deception. Questions meant to make us doubt the goodness of God and blind us to the consequences that will follow if we choose to embrace the deception. The first subtle lie came in the form of the question... Did God really say (Genesis 3:1) ...it was embraced, and sadly is being listened to and embraced by multitudes today who are questioning God on nearly every front. Did God really say...all have sinned and fall short of the glory of God (Romans 3:23)... that the wages of sin is death (Romans 6:23)...that just as man is destined to die once and after that face judgment (Hebrews 9:27)... Did God really say...he will say to those on his left, 'Depart from me, you who are cursed, into the eternal fire prepared for the devil and his angels (Matthew 25:41)...Did God really say...He created man in his own image, in the image of God he created them, male and female (a clear distinction) he created them (Genesis 1:27)... Did God really say...marriage should be honored by all, and the marriage bed kept pure, for God will judge the adulterer and all the sexually immoral (Hebrews 13:4)...Did God really say...that the children of the womb (those who are fearfully and wonderfully knit together in their mother's womb (Psalm 139) are a blessing (Psalm 127:3-5)...children don't miraculously appear as a result of being delivered by a stork and it takes a man and a woman to procreate…Did God really say…you shall not murder (Exodus 20:13)…the killing of innocent children made in the image of God while still in their mother's womb is murder! Did God really say…a woman must not wear men's clothing, nor a man wear woman's clothing (Deuteronomy 22:5)…a man shall not lie with a man as with a woman…marriage should be honored by all and the marriage bed kept pure (Hebrews 13:4)…Did God really say…love the Lord with all your heart, with all your soul, with all your strength, and with all your mind and your neighbor as yourself (Matthew 22:36-40)…Did God really say…unless a man is born again he cannot enter the kingdom of God (John 3:3)…unless you repent and become like little children you cannot enter Heaven (Matthew 18:2-4)…that without holiness no one will see God (Hebrews 12:14)…Did God really say…you shall not take the name of the Lord your God in vain...Did not God demonstrate His love to the world (John 3:16)? God offers this invitation to all…to repentant adulterers, murderers, abortionists, homosexuals, lesbians, thief's, fornicators, blasphemers, etc.… come to me all you who are weary, and burden and I will give you rest (Matthew 11:28-30) …here I am, I stand at the door and knock. If anyone hears my voice and opens the door (the door of our heart) I will come in and eat (have a close intimate relationship) with him and he with me (Revelation 3:20). And to those who do open the door He says…like newborn babies crave pure spiritual milk so that by it you may grow up in your salvation now that you have tasted that the Lord is good.

Christians: pick up your Bible's and read (James 1:22-25) … because God really did say…if anyone is ashamed of me and my words in this adulterous and sinful generation, the Son of man will be ashamed of them when he comes in his Father's glory.

8. Freedom of Speech

What a wonderful gift our founding fathers have given us. A gift they acknowledged comes from our Creator. When it comes to free speech what kind of laws do Korea, Russia, Canada, and other countries have?

Freedom of speech is a principle that supports the freedom of an individual or a community to articulate their opinions and ideas without fear of retaliation, censorship, or legal sanction.

There are approximately 45,000 churches in America. In Bureau County alone there are 43. Our currency says, "In God We Trust". Some of the most important monuments, buildings, and landmarks in Washington, D.C. include religious words, symbols, and imagery. In the United States Capital, the declaration "In God We Trust" is prominently displayed in both the United States House and Senate Chambers. 87% of American households have a Bible in their home.

As Christians are we not allowed to share what God's Word says about marriage, adultery, homosexuality, gender babble, abortion, money and education? Abraham Lincoln made this proclamation, "It is the duty of nations as well as of men to owe their dependency upon the overruling power of God. To confess their sins and transgressions in humble sorrow, yet with assured hope that genuine repentance will lead to mercy and pardon". Abraham Lincoln and our founding fathers were brave men, men whom others wanted to silence.

The etymology of holiday comes from the Old English "holy day". We celebrate Good Friday (Jesus' death) and Easter (His resurrection) and soon we will be celebrating Christmas, the birth of our Savior Jesus Christ. Jesus said, "The Spirit gives life; the flesh counts for nothing. The words I have spoken to you are Spirit and they are life" (John 6:63). America will be in grave danger should we ever lose our freedom of speech. Will America's press like other countries try to silence God Himself as well as the teaching of Jesus (Matthew chapters 5-7)? May it never be! In a recent article about Chester Weger the plural use of the word "pose" was used as well as the word "threat".

The Bible says of Christians, "Have nothing to do with the fruitless deeds of darkness, but rather "expose" them. It is shameful even to mention what the disobedient do in secret" (Ephesians 5:11). The Bible is clear that murder, adultery, homosexuality, divorce, pornography, deception, lying, and stealing, etc. "poses" a "threat" on a society (Proverbs 14:34). If Chester Weger were innocent a great injustice has been done to him. But if guilty and unrepentant a greater punishment awaits him on the Day of Judgment (Matthew 25:41)! Spiritually, even those who are rightfully paying their debt to society by imprisonment can be set free to enter heaven upon their death. God offers compassionate release to all of us (Romans 6:23; 8:1; 1st Peter 3:18) for we are all in need of it. All one need do is genuinely repent (Matthew 18:3) and receive (John 1:12).

9. Yes, Dakota, 'the Christmas story is a true masterpiece'

Dear Editor!
I am 9 years old. Some of my friends tell me that the Christmas story is not true. My daddy says the Christmas story is about the baby Jesus, God's only begotten Son, a messenger of light in this dark world, the promised Messiah. Please give me an honest answer, Mr. Editor, in this dark world filled with so many conflicting messages.
Dakota

Dakota, having been blinded by this scientific technological age, your friends are wrong. Their knowledge has puffed them up with blinding pride! They see so much beauty and miraculous designs in nature but fail to acknowledge the Designer. Rejecting the Christmas story, they become gods in their own eyes.

The heavenly Father gave us the gift of His Son with the offer to restore mankind to the highest place of dignity. His gift is filled with grace and mercy, forgiveness and redemption. Dreary is the heart that rejects this precious gift. Those who do so replace God's sacred gift of marriage and sex with perverted depravity and debauchery, God's awesome creation with the foolish theory of evolution, godly education with an education void of God's moral standards, the sacred gift of life with the killing of the innocent by means of abortion.

Dakota, is their evidence for God and His wonderful Christmas story? Yes! Overwhelming evidence! "Since the creation of the world God's invisible qualities, his eternal power and divine nature have been clearly seen, being understood by what has been made, so that men are without excuse." (Romans 1:20). The Bible is God's special revelation. And the good news, the Gospel it contains, is simple enough to be understood by a child as well as a genius.

Christmas is just the beginning of the story because Jesus did not remain a baby. His story progresses to his miracles and his teachings (doctrines), the Golden Rule and his many proclamations of his deity. The story moves to the cross of Calvary and from there to the grave. But the grave did not bring the story to an end; it leads us to the Easter story, the story where Jesus rose again. It is a never-ending story filled with mystery and love for it speaks of his ascension where he joined the Father up above.

The Christmas story is a true masterpiece! It is a story of miraculous prophesies fulfilled. "The secret things belong to the Lord our God, but the things revealed belong to us and to you, our children, forever." (Deuteronomy 29:29). Some mysteries will remain, but many will be unveiled to those who received this precious gift!

Everybody lives by faith, either in the theory of evolution or the truth as revealed to us in God's Word. So, push aside the curtain of darkness and step into His glorious light, and then "grow in the grace and knowledge of our Lord and Savior Jesus Christ" and join the "wise men who still seek him."

I wrote this letter to the Editor in response to the famous letter by Virginia O'Hanlon and the New York Sun September 21, 1897 editorial response to her letter "Is There a Santa Clause?" It is the most reprinted newspaper editorial in the English language. The editorial response was "Yes, Virginia, there is a Santa Claus".

10. Life is Precious

Jesus loves the little children
Red and yellow, black and white
They are precious in his sight
Jesus loves the little children of the world

To abort something is to stop something in process. To stop a life is murder and now it has become legal in New York to (abort) murder children even after their birth. Pray it never be so in Illinois. I recently went to a mayoral forum so I could be informed on some issues. How well informed are we as Christians today who set under the teaching of God's Word for 52 weeks out of the year about this precious gift called life, its origin, its meaning, and its final destination?

Genesis 1:27 "So God created man in his own image, in the image of God he created him; male and female he created them." Psalm 139:13-14 "For you created my inmost being; you knit me together in my mother's womb. I praise you because I am fearfully and wonderfully made." These verses explain our miraculous intelligent origin by God. We need to teach our children the truth before we send them into a world system that teaches them they evolved from monkeys. What a repulsive, insulting, derogatory portrait of ourselves and our heavenly Father of whom we claim to worship!

Why are we here and how should we live? As Christians Christ should have supremacy in our lives for "He is the image of the invisible God, the firstborn over all creation. For by him all things were created...For God was pleased to have all his fullness dwell in him and through him to reconcile to himself all things." (Colossians 1:15-20)

Titus 2:11-12 "For the grace of God that brings salvation has appeared to all men. It teaches us to say "No" to ungodliness and worldly passions, and to live self-controlled, upright and godly lives in this present age, while we wait for the blessed hope-the glorious appearing of our great God and Savior, Jesus Christ, who gave himself for us to redeem us from all wickedness and to purify for himself a people that are his very own, eager to do what is good." Having been justified this is the sanctification process that follows.

Those who truly receive (John 1:12) and follow (Luke 9:23) Christ, "the King will say, 'Come, you who are blessed by my Father; take your **"inheritance"**, the kingdom prepared for you since the creation of the world." (Matthew 25:31-40) Once one receives Christ into their life, they will start to understand the many wonderful things this **"inheritance"** includes.

There is a priceless value and sacredness to every human being. Science reveals the truth about the miracle of life in the womb. By four weeks the baby's heart is pumping its own blood, having pumped more than one million times. By seven weeks girls now have ovaries and boys have testes. 4,000 of the 4,500 body parts, 90% of what completes an adult, are present by just eight weeks. Indeed, we are fearfully and wonderfully made!

11. Politics are Dirty?

The people throughout the country cried out in anger, why are there so many problems in our land? While grumbling, they were quick to point their fingers at their leaders, crying politics are dirty and so is everyone involved in politics.

Often, when people get angry, they can lose their ability to reason and think clearly. And when one has a cloudy mind, he can at times be easily persuaded to do irrational things.

The Bible says, "In your anger do not sin" (Ephesians 4:26).

From time to time a voice cries out as from a desert with a message for the masses that is meant to prick their consciences, a message that points the finger back at the people themselves. A voice wanting them to recall their history, their roots and the foundation on which their country had been built. But sadly, there are often many younger people who have never been taught the truth about their history and have even been lied to about its origin. So it is a voice that wants all to know, both those who never heard as well as those who had forgotten, about six laws, laws that had been embraced and followed, not by all but by the majority, regardless of religious or ethnic background. Laws that when followed, benefit and bless and even bring joy to the masses though many might not know the origin of these laws. These laws are the last six of God's Ten Commandments. They deal with how man is to relate to his fellow man.

1. Honor your father and mother.
2. Do not murder.
3. Do not commit adultery.
4. Do not steal.
5. Do not give false testimony against your neighbor.
6. Do not covet.

I would hope that most would want to live under the protection these principles provide.

We have also been blessed with a wonderful constitution. John Adams, who was the second president of the United States said, "Our constitution was designed only for a moral and religious people." He understood that each person had to do his or her part by being honest and doing right. Abraham Lincoln said, "Elections belong to the people. It is their decision. If they decide to turn their back on the ire and burn their behinds, then they will just have to sit on their blisters." And Jesus said, "From everyone who has been given much, much will be demanded (required); and from the one who has been entrusted with much, much more will be asked."

Has our consciences become hard and calloused?
We should ask ourselves: Where was I when the orphans needed my support?

...when the hungry needed food?
...when the naked needed clothes?
...when the children needed hugs and kisses?
...when the church doors were opened?
...when the elderly needed visiting?
...where was I on voting day?

Do we not all have responsibilities? None of us can do everything but we all can do something.

12. Political and Spiritual Character Assassination

Nancy Pelosi said the problem with republicans is God, gays and guns. Is she a atheist, a humanist? I am not ashamed to say that I believe in God. True Christians are Christ followers. Jesus said, "Come follow me." But what do we know about Jesus' claims, his character, his disciples, his politics and his expectations of us who claim to follow him today? Read through the book of Proverbs if you wish to know his political views. There have been a lot of dark things coming out of the closet over the past 50 years, socialism, atheism, evolution, amorality, abortion, humanism, supposedly no-fault divorce, homosexuality, etc. It is time that professing Christians come out of their comfortable closets and step into this dark world and be the salt and light that Jesus said his true followers are to be (Matthew 5:13-16). Sadly, many churches fail to place God's standards before their congregations. We hear much about the kind and compassionate Jesus but very little about the bold and courageous Jesus who exposed the spiritual and political corruption of his day as well as each individual person's heart. Why do you think Jesus was crucified? I used to be on the left side of Jesus (Matthew 25:41), the dark side if you will. There is a very clear distinction between the left and the right. Jesus said a city on a hill cannot be hidden.

We have been bombarded by those who oppose the moral standards as set forth in the Bible and yet we have remained silent. If you read the faith chapter (Hebrews chapter 11) you will find these people of faith faced fierce opposition and yet they stood strong.

We can see parallels today with what happened to Jesus in the spiritual and political realm. According to the Mosaic Law, those who falsely accused Jesus (the Son of God) should have themselves been crucified. Let us look at the political and spiritual character assassination of our Lord and Savior Jesus Christ, at the false accusations brought against him.

1. Blasphemy
2. Demon possession
3. Born of fornication
4. Condoning sin by fellowshipping with sinners
5. Sabbath breaker
6. Intemperance
7. Destroy this temple and in three days I will lift it up
8. Perverting the nation
9. Forbidding paying taxes to Caesar
10. Claiming to be a king, a revolutionary
    When asked, Jesus said my kingdom is not of this world.

A broader overview shows at least 33 instances of accusations and criticisms against Christ. The government will never be the Savior of the world. Benjamin Franklin said...I have lived, sir, a long time; and the longer I live the more convincing proofs I see of this truth, that God governs in the affairs of men!...We have been assured, sir, in the sacred Writings, that "except the Lord build the house, they labor in vain who build it."...and I also believe that without His concurring aid we shall succeed in this political building no better than the builders of Babel...

Then he implored the assistance of heaven and its blessing on their deliberations by praying.

13. The Heart of the Christmas Story

Christmas is a true story, an intriguing story, a story loved and accepted and embraced by many for the truth it contains. It is God's love story to mankind. And sadly, it is also a story that has been rejected, secularized and exploited by many. The Christmas story contains many important words such as faith, courage, fear, deception, obedience, angels, joy, love, wonder, peace, relationships and yes, even government officials (yikes!) are included in His story.

The Christmas story is about a person. At the appearing of a Star, wise men traveled from far off lands to bear Him gifts and to honor and worship Him. But king Herod conspired in his "heart" to have the Christ child put to death. The Bible speaks a lot about the "heart". Jesus, speaking of the Pharisees, said, "but I know you. I know that you do not have the love of God in your "hearts" (John 5:42). When Mary heard of the things spoken of Him (Jesus), she treasured them up in her "heart" and pondered them (Luke 2:19). Should we not as Christians treasure up His words and promises in our "hearts"? Jesus came to earth not only to save us but also to strengthen our "hearts" (Isaiah 35:3-5). The Gospel is such good news we should want to "Go tell it on the mountains and over the hills and everywhere! (a Christmas hymn).

Very recently my wife's mother (November 11th, 2020) and her brother (December 11th, 2020) left this earth to be in the presence of the King. Her brother Kevin was not ashamed of the Gospel and his "heart's" desire was that others would come to know Jesus as their Savior. He symbolically would tell it on the mountains and over the hills and everywhere!

A Christian is Christlike when they serve others. My wife is a person who serves others. She has a servant's "heart". Jesus was a person who at the age of twelve amazed the learned teachers in the Temple courts by His understanding (Luke 2:41-52), a person who would fulfill over 100 prophecies made centuries earlier (Luke 24:25-27), a person who had a purpose, a purpose of dying on a cross to provide salvation for people to save them from an eternal Hell. For "since the children have flesh and blood, he too shared in their humanity so that by his death he might destroy him who holds the power of death, that is the devil, and free those who all their lives were held in slavery by their fear of death (Hebrews 2:14-15). He was a person who divided time in two and as a result we have history before Christ and after Christ. "B. C." stands for "before Christ". "A. D." stands for "Anno Domini" Latin for "in the year of the Lord' and refers specifically to the birth of Jesus Christ. Please join your "heart" with mine and others this Christmas and say "Happy birthday" Jesus!

14. Politicians and their Craft

I was impressed by the recent article "The indispensable craft of politicians" by Lee H. Hamilton. I believe it was well written, skillful, if you will. Lee's article mentioned skill, shaking hands, improving one's craft, clergy and one's foe possibly becoming a comrade. But it is just one article and I know little about this gentleman and where he stands on issues such as the killing of the innocent by those who put to death the children of their womb by means of abortion, although it is not unpardonable it is a hideous sin, or where he stands on the Word of God, original sin, redemption, the family, marriage, fornication, homosexuality, adultery, redemption, grace, etc.

It is good for one to strive to improve his craft, but we must beware of craftiness! One's belief, disbelief, inaccurate or distorted view of God and His Word will determine their political outlook, what they stand for or against. And if we want our clergy to correctly handle the word of truth (II Timothy 2:15) these above-mentioned issues should be of utmost importance to Christ followers. "Righteousness exalts a nation, but sin is a disgrace to any people" (Proverbs 14:34).

When one rejects Christ and his teachings, he then chooses to do what is right in his own eyes much like in the days of judges (Judges 17:6; 21:25). I myself was once God's enemy but Christ came to reconcile sinners, (God's enemies or foe) which would include all of us, back to God by shedding his blood, making peace, friendship and camaraderie possible between God and man (II Corinthians 5:18). This is God's offer of grace to mankind.

It's OK to be cautious with whom we shake hands because God himself asks, "What does righteousness have to do with unrighteousness? Or what does light have to do with darkness? (II Corinthians 6:14). Remember the scene when George Bailey shook hands with Mr. Potter but was repulsed and withdrew his hand and wiped it off. Or the movie "Frost/Nixon" where Jim Reston said he would not shake hands with the President. I imagine that many shook hands with Bernie Madoff in whom they trusted.

Jesus asked, "I have shown you many good works from the Father. For which of these do you stone me? The Bible testifies that abortion, lying, adultery, homosexuality, fornication, spousal abuse, etc. is evil. Jesus said, "The world cannot hate you, but it hates me because I testify that what it does is evil" (John 7:7). Jesus at times used harsh words but only after much patience and reasoning from the very Scriptures that those who hated him had in their possession. There are "politicians" and "clergy" on the left and the right who identify with a religion but who do not follow Christ or obey his teachings. "…they have a form of godliness but deny the power thereof' (II Timothy 3:5). Yes, one should be cautious with whom they choose to shake hands!

15. The Sky is Falling!!

The greatest fear that looms over mankind is the fear of death. I imagine that most, if they had a choice in the matter of their death, would prefer to die peacefully in their sleep after having lived a long healthy prosperous life. I myself have experienced fear before and even throughout my Christian walk. There are different reasons for this. First, I still have a sin nature, it has not been eradicated. Second, as a Christian I have a formidable enemy. Third, as a Christian one starts out as a babe in Christ and in need of protection because there are roaring lions looking for someone to devour (I Peter 5:8).

Peer pressure is synonymous with fear pressure. There are two kinds of fear. There is a healthy fear and there is an unhealthy fear. When ten, my granddaughter faced her fear of heights and went on a five run zip line! Imaginary phobias can cripple people. There is a huge difference between chihuahua's and police dogs on the trail of a criminal, daddy long legs and brown recluse spiders, gardener snakes and black mambas. Sometimes it is wise to be fearful.

Someone once said the greatest power in the world is not nuclear warheads with their capability to destroy the world (that's a fearful thought) but the power of choosing where we will spend eternity, our freedom of choice. And consequences follow our choices.

There are many "Chicken Little's" out there and today many are asking, "Are we in the Last Days" or "Is the Sky Falling?" My response to such questions is, whether we are or not, should we as Christians be idle and disengaged? The problem is not so much that the sky is falling, but rather, that mankind has fallen.

Sin is a universal reality. It isn't unique to just one people group. "For all have sinned and fall short of the glory of God (Romans 3:23). The word sin has almost vanished from America's vocabulary! Solomon said, "The fear of the LORD is the beginning of knowledge, but fools despise wisdom and discipline" (Proverbs 1:7). Robert B. Strimple says to fear the Lord "consists of awe, reverence, adoration, honor, worship, confidence, love, and thankfulness." It can also mean fear of God's judgment. "Do not be afraid of those who can kill the body but cannot kill the soul. Rather, be afraid of the One who can destroy both soul and body in hell" (Matthew 10:28).

What we need is for the truth to fall down from Heaven and hit us on the head, and then, after God has gotten our attention, we need to ask God to let His truth penetrate our hearts. We hear much of the love of God but little of a God who judges sin. Remember Noah's flood. Remember Sodom and Gomorrah. Remember the purpose and reason Jesus died upon the cross (I Peter 3:18) and the purpose of Communion and be thankful! "For God so loved the world... (John 3:16).

16. The Plumb Line and the Pendulum

Congress shall make no law respecting an establishment of religion...75% of Americans identify with a Christian religion, yet because there is negligence in teaching sound doctrine multitudes are ignorant of biblical truths (1st Timothy 4:15-16; II Timothy 4:3; Titus 1:9; 2:1).

God has given us a Plumb Line. But sadly, much of our culture and many churches no longer have an awareness of the Plumb Line. "Be perfect, therefore, as your heavenly Father is perfect". Have you ever scratched your head and said, "What! You've got to be kidding me"? Nicodemus scratched his head. Nick said what! Can a man enter a second time into his mother's womb and be born? (John Chapter 3).

The gospel is simple. Man sinner, God holy, Christ Redeemer. Theology is sometimes deep, difficult, and complex. Man is sinful, ignorant, and sometimes stupidly rebellious. God said, come, let us reason together, though your sins are like scarlet they shall be white as snow, though they are red like crimson they shall be as wool. Salvation is threefold. Salvation = justification, sanctification, glorification. Theology explained. Justification, one stands before God as (perfect) from the moment one "repents" and believes and receives Christ (born again). Sanctification is the process of growing in holiness (set apart for a sacred purpose) after being justified (II Peter 1:3-8). Glorification is the final stage of ones salvation. Justification = saved from the penalty of sin.

Sanctification = being saved from the power of sin. Glorification = saved from the very presence of sin.

God's standard is "be perfect". Christ is the Plumb Line (the Perfect One). Our repentance and faith in him and his finished work is our justification. The process of sanctification is our experience as we grow in God's grace as we await glorification.

We are the Pendulum. Jesus balanced truth and love perfectly. We, on the other hand, oscillate from one side of the Plumb Line to the other (Romans 7:7-25). Our walk goes from birth to growth to maturity; we are a work in progress (sanctification). He who begun a good work in you is faithful to bring it to completion (glorification). After our justification we are now God's workmanship created in Christ Jesus to do works of grace, again sanctification, we do not earn salvation!

A few other neglected biblical doctrines... Life (when it starts, Psalm 139)...Gender (male and female)...Biblical Marriage (one man, one woman)...Creation (not evolution)...the Doctrine of the Covenants...of Repentance....of Adoption...of Reconciliation...of Christian Ethics...Divine Inspiration...Holy Spirit...Trinity...Eternal Security...Last Things...etc.

Jesus said, "Blessed are those who hunger and thirst for righteousness, for they will be filled." Are you saved or religious? Ask yourself, "Do I have a hunger and thirst for truth and holiness? Am I growing in love and godly character? If the truth is taught (biblical doctrines), people will have the opportunity to make an informed decision and choose to accept or reject the claims of Jesus and the Salvation that He offers. Jesus said, "Feed my sheep."

17. Sex, Scandal, and Sin

If all our past thoughts were recorded and then brought out in the open for all to see and then judged by the standard as set forth by Jesus, all of us would be arrested and imprisoned. "You have heard it said, 'Do not murder, but I tell you anyone who is angry with his brother will be subject to judgment. And anyone who says, 'You fool!' will be in danger of the fire of hell. You have heard it said, 'Do not commit adultery.' But I tell you, anyone who looks at a woman lustfully commits adultery in his heart" —- Jesus.

Bill Clinton, Jimmy Carter, Donald Trump, King David, me, you, God's Word clearly states that all have sinned and that the wages of sin is death (the death penalty). The Bible speaks of two alternative destinies after one departs this life. The reason we do not hear the word sin used in the public arena is because we would be placing the true moral standard back where it belongs, with God.

Murder is a crime punishable by death in 30 states, yet we sit by quietly as our country endorses the murder of innocent babies while still in the womb or during the birth of the child. Yes, partial birth abortion has finally been made illegal but shrewd and devious people have found a way around it. Are you familiar with how "doctors are using lethal drugs to kill babies in the womb, so the baby is killed before its delivery? It allows doctors to circumvent the partial-birth law, or at least the spirit of it, because the intent of the law is to prevent babies being aborted that would otherwise be able to live outside of the womb." Why are these children being unjustly led to the slaughter? To abort something is to stop something in progress. And to stop a life is murder! Jesus said we are not to judge hypocritically; he did not mean we are not to make intelligent judgments. What are our children learning about sex in our schools, our churches, and our homes? It seems we have forgotten that children are conceived as a result of two people having sexual intercourse. What is safe sex? Abstinence until marriage (God's standard) is the only true way to have 100% assurance of safe sex. There are sins of commission and sins of omission. Jesus said, speaking of Christians, "You are the salt of the earth." Is salt being omitted from our pulpits? The loss of a father through death, divorce, indifference or willful ignorance of God's Word and the breakdown of the family is attributing to much of our problems we are facing today. When it comes to the education of our children, we as a nation have strayed from the path of understanding. "It is not the healthy who need a doctor, but the sick. I have not come to call the righteous, but sinners to repentance" —-Jesus.

18. Seed Planters

This letter is in response to the recent articles (battery charges while under the influence of drugs--indictments--meth bust--opioids crisis--) and their questions and statements on marijuana, child pornography etc.--Today we are seeing the results of seeds planted years ago. Over 70,000 opioids deaths in just one year! Thankfully, there are many who purpose in their hearts to plant good seeds in our community. How have we come to the place that we need A.L.I.C.E. (Alert, Lockdown, Inform, Counter, Evacuate) in our schools? How ironic that we have to set aside money for public education on substance abuse after others allow the abuse and encourage it in the first place.

Jesus said, "Unless a kernel of wheat falls to the ground and dies it remains a single seed. But if dies it produces many seeds" (John 12:24). We have many farmers and many churches in our community. Some understand the concept of reaping and sowing while others seem ignorant of it. Flimsy and feeble statements such as "Like it or not it is already here" and "only good things would come from a dispensary" are bad seed statements. "You have a choice to do the right thing" (for the sake of our children) and "We're a community that tries to stay ahead of the game with drug prevention" are good seed statements by Tom Root. You have the mayor saying you could fund the police, the very ones who are trying to prevent and take a stand against the bad seeds being planted that cause the problem in the first place. It is like saying let us start a fire, exploit it and then use the money to put out the fires we create! Pointing out that the money made could help fund those who are trying to put the fire out is an oxymoron statement. You have a former Police chief saying guide our children in the right direction and the mayor who seems to be agreeing with the statement "Like it or not it is already here" and allowing the problem to continue to worsen instead of embracing preventative measures. We do not want to be a community hiding behind a facade, an outward appearance that is maintained to conceal a less pleasant or less credible reality.

"Little children say, and do as they hear others say, and see others do; so easily do they imitate; and therefore, great care must be taken to set them good examples, and no bad ones. Children will learn of those that are with them, either to curse and swear, or pray and praise" —-Matthew Henry. An ounce of prevention is worth a pound of cure! The question "Who do we have a moral obligation too" is a good soul-searching question put before each one of us. It is God who has given us a moral compass. Romans 14:12 "So then, each of us will give an account of ourselves to God."

19. Should not God's Voice be Heard Today?

A resounding yes to the question! Of course it should. "Wisdom calls aloud in the streets, she raises her voice in the public squares; at the head of the noisy streets, she cries out, in the gateways of the city she makes her speech (Proverbs 1:20-21). This would include the streets of Bureau County.

There are many issues being discussed and debated today. When I was in school, we had a class that discussed current events and we also had a history class. Christians have a right and a responsibility to speak their voice on issues facing us today, such as abortion, homosexuality, how God defines a family, religious liberty, socialism, gender babble, education, how God's principles apply in politics, accountability, repentance, etc.

These issues speak a lot about America's conscience or lack of it, they are heart issues. We often long for peace and tranquility. One of the titles of the Holy Spirit is Comforter. What are some of His other attributes and purposes? Jesus said, "When He comes, He will convict the world of guilt in regard to sin and righteousness and judgment" (John 16:8). Matthew Henry said, "The coming of the Holy Spirit was absolutely necessary to the carrying on of Christ's interests on earth."

Man has opinions, but it is the Holy Spirit who convicts the conscience and softens the human heart, "For the wages of sin is death, but the gift of God is eternal life" (Romans 6:23). Christians belong to Christ that we might bear fruit to God (Romans 7:4).

Christians rely on God's Word as their source of guidance and 75% of American's polled profess to be Christian.

Jesus often answered people's questions with a question, his questions are of the utmost importance for "Righteousness exalts a nation, but sin is a disgrace to any people" (Proverbs 14:34). Conviction is a good thing although very uncomfortable at times as we grow through the sanctifying process for "No discipline seems pleasant at the time, but painful. Later on, however, it produces a harvest of righteousness and peace to those who have been trained by it" (Hebrews 12:11).

Are you a book reader? There are 27 books that we as Christians should put on our list of books to read for there are 27 separate books in the New Testament consisting of 260 chapters. A reasonable, attainable goal is to read one chapter a day. This means one can read through the New Testament easily each year. Jesus said, "Man does not live on bread alone, but on every word that comes from the mouth of God" (Matthew 4:4).

Jesus gathered around him ordinary people, fishermen, despised tax collectors, prostitutes, many with a willingness to repent and learn. The Bible makes a clear distinction between good and evil, righteousness and unrighteousness, male and female. Ephesians 5:14 says, "Wake up, O sleeper, rise from the dead, and Christ will shine on you."

20. Socialism

Having listened to different Democrats and President Obama talk about equal wealth and socialism, I did some checking and came across an article about an economics professors' class that had insisted that Obama's socialism worked and that no one would be poor, and no one would be rich, a great equalizer.

The professor then told them they would have an experiment in his class on Obama's plan...All grades will be averaged, and everyone will receive the same grade; so, no one will fail, and no one will receive an A... (Substituting grades for dollars—something closer to home and more readily understood by all).

After the first test, the grades were averaged, and everyone got a B. The students that studied hard were upset, and the students who studied little were happy. As the second test rolled around, the students who studied little had studied even less, and the ones who studied hard decided they wanted a free ride too, so they studied little.

The second test average was a D! No one was happy.

When the third test rolled around, the average was an F.

As the tests proceeded, the scores never increased as bickering, blame and name-calling all resulted in hard feelings and no one would study for the benefit of anyone else. To their great surprise, all failed, and the professor told them that socialism would ultimately fail because when the reward is great, the effort to succeed is great; but when government takes all the reward away no one will try or want to succeed. It could not be any simpler than that. These are possibly the five best sentences you will ever read and all applicable to this experiment:

1. You cannot legislate the poor into prosperity by legislating the wealthy out of prosperity.
2. What one person receives without working for, another person must work for without receiving.
3. The government cannot give to anybody anything the government does not first take from somebody else.
4. You cannot multiply wealth by dividing it.
5. When half the people get the idea that they do not have to work because the other half is going to take care of them, and when the other half gets the idea that it does no good to work because somebody else is going to get what they work for, that is the beginning of the end of any nation.

I now know what they are talking about when they talk about socialism, and I hope this helps others understand it also.

This letter to the Editor was written by Raymond White of Ohio, Ill on 1/7/2016 when Washington was at its worse. He also made the following statement about those in power at the time. They should "Stop thinking about their personal political futures and what they can get out of it, but what is best for the country—-not best for them."

I (Ted) would encourage you to read the teaching by Jesus found in The Parable of the Talents from Matthew 25:14-30." Abraham Lincoln said our government was to be a servant to the people and we as a people were not to be a people subservient to the government. Jesus spoke of personal responsibility as did Abraham Lincoln in his Gettysburg Address—- "government of the people, by the people, for the people."

21. The Touch of Christmas

Have you read the poem or listened to the song "Touched by the Master's Hand" about an old violin deemed worthless until placed in the hands of a master violinist? If not, I would encourage you to Google it.

Ah, Christmas, "Tis the season to be jolly" because "It's the most wonderful time of the year", unless, of course, your "Grandma got run over by a reindeer"!

What is the real purpose of Christmas? Is it a holiday or a holy day, a time to worship or a time to be relational, a time to give or a time to receive? Is about Santa Claus or about Jesus? I believe all are true.

When I was a young and immature Christian, I was anti-Santa Claus. At times we as Christians can be very un-Christlike. When Jesus' immature disciples reprimanded the people, those who were bringing little children to have Jesus "touch" them, Jesus became indignant and rebuked his disciples. Being somewhat more mature and more Christlike today, I would invite Santa in for milk and cookies and, more important, I would share the Gospel with him.

Those of us who understand the real meaning of salvation, having been "touched" by the Master's hand, are called to feed the hungry, clothe the naked, give drink to those who thirst, visit those in prison, invite strangers into our homes (Matthew 25:35-36), and minister to the poor, the crippled, the blind and the lame (Luke 14:21).

Some, feeling the "touch" of the Master's hand through us, might come to Christ for salvation also. Yes, we enter church to worship, but the church is also a place that is supposed to equip the body of believers in holy living, "for without holiness no one will see the Lord" (Hebrews 12:14) and prepare them to go out and serve. Christians are no longer under the condemnation of the law, but we are to uphold it (Romans 3:31). It is the ceremonial laws that have been done away with, not the moral laws and standards that God has set in place.

When Mary kissed the baby Jesus, she kissed the face of God (Mark Lowry), Matthew 1:21-23). A kiss on the forehead or cheek is a form of "touch", expressing our love or a form of greeting, but how ugly it was for Judas to betray Jesus with a kiss. For many, Christmas is a narcissistic holiday, a betraying of the real meaning of Christmas!

How many of us, even as Christians, have withheld "touch" from those we love when we were angry, but after apologies were given and forgiveness received, the warmth of touch returned? Jesus did not have to touch people in order to heal them, but often used this method to do so. He even touched those whom his disciples tried to silence (Luke 18:39).

Spiritually, we are all in need of a touch from the Master's hand. Do you love the Christ of Christmas? Are you touching others with His love?

22. Show Tolerance

To the Editor
In response to Tuesday's (March 24) Letter to the Editor, 'Shame, shame, shame," by (Mr. anonymous) of Dalzell: In the last election, there was no question about "getting rid of Obama care." Sure, some candidates ran on that platform, but if they did and it was not brought in front of Congress then that is the candidate's fault, and can be voted out by the public, next election. Second, where did you get the information that marriage should be between a man and a woman only? I don't believe most Americans agree with that. It might be in the Bible, but this country was founded on religious freedom and separation of church and state. If you are against that, then may I suggest you don't marry within your same sex. Same as abortion; if you don't like it, don't get one. If you don't like alcohol, then don't drink it. But don't take away the rights of others who have beliefs contrary to yours. That is what the war on terrorists is all about! Not forcing others into beliefs that you don't agree with.

Third, the United States Supreme Court doesn't have the power to change what is written in the Bible. It has no jurisdiction over that. It only rules on constitutional issues. So, you don't have to worry about that and the Fourth Commandment. There are Muslim extremists and Christian extremists that wish to change the life we lead; please don't be one of those. We can all live in peace and harmony if we stop trying to make everyone follow certain beliefs but show tolerance toward each other.

Mr. Anonymous #2
Princeton

My Response to Mr. Anonymous; You Sly Guy!

Recently I have been reading many articles in the paper that go far beyond just being sad. Suicide, drug abuse, bullying, depression, and poverty on the rise. Is it a bully's right to bully? I do not think a person thinks it is their "right" to commit suicide. My brother committed suicide and it affected all of us who loved him. I do not think that people who are addicted to drugs think of it as being their right. Children who come from broken homes and bullied children will struggle with depression, a form of grief. But one's grief can become unhealthy and turn into a sickness. Many try to deaden their pain through drugs, alcohol, or suicide. And divorce hurts everyone involved. It is usually accompanied by financial loss, insecurities, anger and depression. This letter is a response to Thursday's (April 2) Letter to the Editor "Show tolerance" and its subject matter, marriage between a man and a woman, the Bible, abortion, alcohol, voting, religious freedom and separation of church and state, and forcing others into beliefs that you do not agree with. Mr. Anonymous #2, you sly guy. Separation between church and state is not in our constitution! Our founding fathers had to fight with physical weapons in order to gain freedom from England, but they used weapons of another kind to establish the freedoms that our nation has enjoyed now into its third century. They used words! They gave us our constitution and it is based on and rooted in the principles from the Bible, the Scriptures. There was no separation of these biblical principles when they wrote the constitution! Those whose standards and morals that differ from yours do not have the right to force their beliefs on anyone. Every law legislates someone's morality, a particular worldview. All people who can vote are free to vote their conscience. I do not agree with the saying that "if you don't like alcohol don't drink it" as if to say your freedom to drink does not have an effect on others. Over 30,000 car deaths each year and thousands more crippled or left with brain damage for life. Divorce, drugs, killing innocent children by abortion, fornication, crack cocaine, texting while driving, pornography are all lifestyles with consequences. Homosexuality is a sin. It was not my particular sin. My following sin list is incomplete to be sure. Drunkenness, fornication, (sex outside of marriage), occasional unkindness and rudeness, apathy and indifference. The Bible says that those who live like this will not inherit the Kingdom of God (Heaven) II Corinthians 6:9-11. We are not in need of "tolerance" but repentance and to be open to receive God's gift of grace and mercy. Understanding that there are those who may disagree with us who believe in a different way, I hope that they themselves will apply what they say they believe and show the same "tolerance" to us that they say we should show them.

23. What Difference does it Make!!!?

Under her watch, just three short months after the killing of four American men at Benghazi, throwing her hands in the air, Hillary Clinton angrily proclaimed "What difference does it make?!!!" Jesus said, "For out of the overflow of the heart the mouth speaks" (Matthew 12:34). Hillary's words revealed what was in her heart, bringing upon herself shame and disgrace. But what about we who claim to be followers of Jesus? You have heard the saying, "Actions speak louder than words". Biblically, we as Christians are to use both actions and words. Being good does not make a person righteous. Going to church does not make a person a Christian. Nor does mere intellectual assent.

Each of us should ask ourselves the following questions.
What difference does our constitution make?
What difference does it make concerning the kind of education our children receive?
What difference does it make if we stand up for justice?
What difference does it make if we are apathetic?
...voting would fall under the last two questions.
What difference does it make if we are a people of principle or see ourselves as being insignificant?
What difference does it make if we are pseudo-Christians or true followers of Christ?

Letters To The Editor

What difference does it make if we are heading toward orderliness or chaos?
What difference does it make if we are courageous or cowardly? Look at Revelation 21:8
What difference do our priorities make?
What difference does thirty minutes make in our daily routine?
What difference does it make if we read our Bible and pray? Think thirty minutes.
Jesus' answer to these questions is that it will make an eternal difference.

Our nation is facing a moral dilemma. But gloom and doom does not need to be our perspective. The problems that we face are problems of the heart. Including apathy, indifference and fear. At this point in our nation, we still have the freedom to vote and make a difference. Biblically, a family unit consists of a marriage between a man and a woman. There is a clear distinction between a male and female. A mother's womb should be a haven from outside intrusion, not a mortuary as a result of killing an innocent child. History shows a pendulum swinging right then to the left and back to the right again. It is time for it to swing back to the right. Many adults are influencing and encouraging our youth to defy God and celebrate sin. Paul, inspired by the Holy Spirit of God, wrote, "Wake up, O sleeper, rise up from the dead, and Christ will shine on you." (Ephesians 5:14). Will history look back on us as a people who stood up and made a difference for the future of our children and grandchildren or will it look upon us as a generation who brought upon itself shame and disgrace because of our silence? What difference will you make?

24. Sex, Who makes the Rules?

I talked with a missionary friend yesterday and he shared this principle with me. "If something is true, even if no one believes it, it is still true. Or "If something isn't true and everyone believes it, it still isn't true." God created man and woman to complement one another and to procreate. He made sex to be pleasurable. He made it to be between a man and a woman (Genesis 1: and Mark 10:6). He made it to be within the boundaries of marriage (Hebrews 13:4). And He even made it a mystical union of Christ and the church (Ephesians 5:31-32). Mark Twain once said something along this line: It is not the things in the Bible that I do not understand that bother me, it is the things I do understand. Once we hear the truth what are we going to do with it? Acknowledge it, reject it, twist it, or try to skirt around it? I enjoyed the pleasures of pornography for a time, but later found it left me addicted and unfulfilled. After becoming a Christian, I did not enjoy the war that took place and still does at times between my flesh and God's spirit (Romans 7:14-25). Today, many people are making sexual decisions without a passing thought of seeking the revealed truth in God's Word. Oh, that all would come to "know" and have a desire to "do" the truth with their gift of sexuality! That the pastors who were asked to speak up on the subject would do so, knowing that one day they will be held accountable before a holy and just God (James 3:1). And then there are those who proclaim to be spokespersons for God who twist it to for their own agenda

Letters To The Editor

leading to their own destruction (II Peter 3:16). Jesus accepts into his church sinners of all kinds, prostitutes, murderers, homosexuals, thief's, pornographers, drunkards, and even those who have been abusive. But he never puts his stamp of approval on their lifestyles. Those who wanted acceptance into his kingdom needed to turn from the darkness of their sin and turn toward him who said he was the light (John 8:12). They, like those in the church today, needed to "widen or spread the understanding" of their sin and turn from it. Jesus did not call people to a religion, but to be a Christ follower. When this happens, "There will be more light, more truth to be revealed in God's word". I too, believe that God loves all people equally, even the worst of sinners. As for our minds, Paul wrote the following. "Therefore, I urge you brothers, in view of God's mercy, to offer your bodies as living sacrifices, holy and pleasing to God, this is your spiritual act of worship. Do not conform any longer to the pattern of this world but be transformed by the renewing of your mind (Romans 12:1-2).

This letter was a response to someone who held a different view on sex contrary to the Word of God.

25. Muddied Waters

In the "Three faiths, one God" article, the bold print title immediately jumped off the page and simultaneously my mind was impressed with the thought, "One God, three Persons!" Father, Son, and Holy Spirit. Christianity is unique from all other religions. In fact, each religion is unique onto itself. They all make personal claims and reject the claims of others. Christianity is about a loving, personal God who wants a relationship with those whom He created in His own image. But what all people, regardless of any religious affiliation have in common is that we are all sinners.

Romans 5:6-9 says: "You see, at just the right time, when we were still powerless, Christ died for the ungodly. Very rarely will anyone die for a righteous man, though for a good man someone might possibly dare to die. But God demonstrates his own love for us in this: while we were still sinners, Christ died for us."

Romans 5:1 says that a sinner can have peace with God through reconciliation. Not merely a subjective feeling (peace of mind) but primarily an objective status, a new relationship with God. Once we were his enemies, but if we repent of our sins and put our faith in what Christ did on the cross, we are no longer his enemies but become his friends. In that sense, Christianity is not a religion but a relationship.

Today, the reality of sin seems to be doubted by many. In order to know what is right or what is wrong we need to look to God's

Letters To The Editor

Word as our standard. Who likes to be lied to or be deceived? Yet the lies we tell ourselves are the most dangerous. "I'm not so bad." "Just one bite won't hurt." "I'll just take one look." "Just one drink won't hurt." Our actions have consequences!

In and of myself, apart from Christ, I am that bad. Eating healthy has been and still is a struggle for me. And I know from experience that one look can lead to another and then another and another. The "just one look" lie is something I still have to keep in check. The first time I inhaled a cigarette was not a pleasant experience, but I wanted to fit in with my peers, so I got past it. My first beer was hard to swallow but eventually I became a very efficient drinker and as a result I was jailed 8 times, had my stomach pumped once and caused much pain and brokenness to others and myself. Your sin list may not be as bad as mine, but you do have one. That does not mean you are "all bad", but it does mean you are not "all good". We all have impurities. Revelation 21:27 says nothing impure will enter Heaven. Our purity comes from Christ alone. There were subtle deceptions in the article, and many in the presentation of the "Three faiths, one God." The three religions share far more differences than similarities! Beware of muddied waters!

26. The Book

To the Editor: In response to "Freedom to read".
Who would not want to read the greatest book ever written… the bestselling book of all history…the first book printed on Gutenberg's 1455 invention of the printing press…a book filled with true and exciting stories for all ages…that has inspired thousands of psalms, hymns, spiritual songs and poems…a book used as a benchmark by which all other books can be measured…that's been translated in over 150 languages…that contains the four Gospels (gospel means good or joyful message)…a book of miracles…a book of fulfilled prophecies (hundreds were fulfilled in the first coming of Jesus)…a book that has gone by several different names… "The Good Book" …" The Holy Scriptures" … "The Sacred Writings" … "The Book" … "The Holy Bible"? Ah! …a beautiful book. After a study of over three thousand documents over a ten- year period it was the one book found to be the most quoted by our Founding Fathers who, by the way, also established "The American Bible Society". It was the book and the principles within on which our Founding Father's established our constitution and the laws of our land. Did you know that the word "separation" and the word "church" and the word "state" are not even found in our constitution? This book has given us our rich heritage. This Bible is the book on which the president of the United States of America is sworn in on when he "swears to uphold our constitution!! It was this book that the idea of our three branches

Letters To The Editor

of government and tax exemption for the churches came. It was this book that gave us our morals and principles and strong economic stability we enjoyed as a nation before their removal from public schools in 1962 and 1963. A couple of years ago I heard the saying "The gate test". A test by which to test the goodness of a country. Are people trying to enter into a country or leave it (think Mexico and other countries)? The Bible, on which our president is sworn in on is banned in over 50 other countries. The Bible places the highest value on the family. Husbands are to love, honor and protect their wives. Wives are to respect their husbands. This provides a safe and healthy environment for their children and is the foundation for a strong and healthy nation. This book gives strong warnings! It condemns lust, greed, hate, fornication, adultery, homosexuality, drunkenness, and other sinful practices but offers love, grace, mercy, and forgiveness to those willing to receive it. People of faith are not "closed minded" for wanting to protect our children from materials damaging to their physical, emotional and spiritual health. For the glory of God and for our own sake let us stand strong once again on the principles found in "The Book".

27. The Heart of America

How appropriate to write an article on the heart at this time. Seven days ago (November 4th, 2020) I had an attack on my physical heart, a muscle that weighs approximately 10 ounces. My first heart attack, hopefully my last. But this newsletter has to do with the heart of which the Bible references over 825 times. It is clear that God places much emphasis on our hearts!

The motto on American currency is "In God we trust". Incoming presidents raise their right hand and place their left hand on a Bible while taking the oath of office. Some of them actually believe in God and take the oath seriously! It is estimated that there are 20 million Bibles sold in America each year and approximately nine out of 10 households have a Bible.

There are many idioms for the word heart. The "Heartland" of America is associated with mainstream or traditional values, such as conservative political and religious ideals. The term "heartland" often evokes imagery of rural farms with their abundant flowing fields of golden wheat. Think of the lyrics of the beloved patriotic song, "America the Beautiful".

These traditional values and conservative and religious ideals have been under attack at their very core, their heart if you will. In other words, there has been an ongoing attack on the heart of America! The Scriptures reveal God's love and His heart in the person of Jesus Christ (John 14:9).

If one wants to know the heart of God then all one needs to do is look at Jesus of who it was said, "is destined to cause the falling and rising of many so the thoughts of many hearts will be revealed" (Luke 2:34-35). "Men will be judged by their hearts, their thoughts concerning Christ" (Matthew Henry).

I believe Abraham Lincoln clearly exposed and powerfully addressed the heart of America in his Thanksgiving Proclamation. "It is the duty of nations as well as of men, to owe their dependence upon the overruling power of God, to confess their sins and transgressions, in humble sorrow, yet with assured hope that genuine repentance will lead to mercy and pardon; and to recognize the subline truth, announced in the Holy Scriptures, that those nations only are blessed whose God is the Lord", he spoke of our nation at the time as a people who "have forgotten God."

"The Word of God is living and active, sharper than any double-edge sword; it penetrates even to dividing soul and spirit, joints and marrow; it judges the thoughts and attitudes of the heart" (Hebrews 4:12). Today we would say, "It cuts to the heart". A good prayer for all who profess to know and love Jesus would be this short prayer by the psalmist: "May the words of my mouth and the meditation of my heart be pleasing in your sight, O Lord, my rock and my redeemer" (Psalm 19:14).

28. If I were a Christian

A contrast to Paul Harvey's, (you may want to google it) "If I were the devil."

If I were a Christian… if I called myself a Christian, I would want to be clear of what it means to be a biblical Christian, I would want to be clear about what Jesus meant when he said, "you must be born again" (John chapter 3) and if in fact such an occurrence had taken place in my life. So, I would ask myself the following questions to see if there was any evidence to confirm my profession that I was indeed a Christian. _First,_ have I understood my sinfulness (Romans 3:23) and God's standard of perfection (Romans 5:8) needed for one to enter into heaven? _Second_, have I understood that my sin carries a penalty (Romans 6:23) and separates me from God? _Third_, have I understood my need to repent (Luke 13:3; Matthew 18:3) and my need to be reconciled (II Corinthians 5:18) to God as announced and proclaimed by both John the Baptist and Jesus Christ? _Forth_, have I understood that faith in Christ's atoning sacrifice on the cross is the standard of perfection (Isaiah 53:5-6) needed as set forth by God the Father? _Fifth_, have I understood that my good works (Isaiah 64:6) cannot gain me entrance into heaven and that salvation is a free gift of grace (Ephesians 2:8-9) and grace alone, a gift received by faith? _Sixth_, have I understood that once I have accepted this gift, I am now God's workmanship created in Christ Jesus to do good works (Ephesians 2:10)? Someone once said, *"We need to teach grace before commitment, because grace understood and embraced will always lead to commitment, but commitment required will always lead to legalism?* <u>Seventh</u>, have I understood what it means to be a Christ follower, a follower of the Prince of Peace?

The following evidence, or fruit, should be evident "If I were a Christian." *If I were a Christian,* there should be a desire in my heart to share the gospel (Romans 1:16-18) with others either by personally sharing my faith and or through my giving by supporting ministries. Jesus would call this "being a (Matthew 4:19) fisher of men." *If I were a Christian,* I would have a desire to walk (John 14:23-24) in obedience to Jesus' teaching. *If I were a Christian,* I would be a lamp in this dark world (Matthew 5:14-16) so that others could light their candle from my lamp so that they too would have a light for their path as they journey through this life. *If I were a Christian,* I would strive always (Acts 24:16) to keep my conscience clear before God and men, realizing that through the sanctifying process I would need to confess my sins and accept (I John 1:8-10) his ongoing faithfulness to forgive me once I have confessed them. *If I were a Christian,* I would set my mind and heart (Colossians 3:1-4) on things above not on worldly things. *If I were a Christian,* I would try not to be neglectful in putting on the full armor of God, knowing that I have an enemy who, though he is not able to snatch me out of my Saviors (John 10:25-30) or my Father's hand, he will constantly try to render me (Ephesians 6:10-18) ineffective in God's kingdom work. *If I were a Christian,* realizing that I have not yet attained perfection, I would daily try to forget what is behind me and I would press forward (Philippians 3:12-14) toward the goal to win the prize for which God has called me heavenward in Christ Jesus. *If I were a Christian,* I would understand from the very beginning that I was a work in progress so I would make every effort to add to my faith goodness; and to goodness, knowledge; and to knowledge, self-control, and to self-control, perseverance; and to perseverance, godliness; and to godliness, brotherly kindness; and to brotherly kindness, love. For by so doing, I would possess these qualities in increasing measure (II Peter 1:5-11) and they would help to keep me from being ineffective and unproductive in my knowledge of my Lord Jesus Christ. *If I were a Christian,* I would strive to be humble, realizing I have no room for arrogance or spiritual pride because at one time I too was foolish, disobedient, deceived and enslaved (Titus 3:13) by all kinds of passions and pleasures, living in malice and envy, being hated and hating others. *If I were a Christian* I would pray for the pastors in my community and those in my own church, and for the leaders of my country that they too (I Timothy 2:1-4) would ask themselves these same questions. My prayer would be that they would believe that all Scripture is God-breathed, not just some of it. And that it is useful for teaching, rebuking, correcting (II Timothy 3:16) and training in righteousness, so that the man of God may be thoroughly equipped for every good work. Having become a Christian a number of years ago, I now realize and have come to know that when the kindness and love of God my Savior appeared, he saved me, not because of righteous (Titus 3:4-7) things that I have done, but because of his mercy. That he saved me through the washing of rebirth and renewal by the Holy Spirit, whom he poured out on me generously through Jesus Christ my Savior, so that, having been justified by his grace, I have become an heir having the hope of eternal life. *Since I have that blessed assurance that I am now a Christian,* this is the path that I will continue to walk as I follow Christ.

About the Author; Ted Roberts

There are those who say they do not have a dramatic or exciting conversion testimony. But I disagree. When any lost sinner comes to faith in Christ it creates joy in Heaven! Jesus said in Luke 10:15 that "there is rejoicing in the presence of the angels of God over one sinner who repents". I myself was born a son of an alcoholic, a man who endured much pain and brokenness and heartache in his life. His 8-month pregnant wife (my mother) died a day after her 25th birthday. He spent 43 years in a Veterans hospital. As a teenager I did not respond well to my lot in life. I was bitter and filled with self-pity and I myself became an alcoholic. The Bible says, speaking of all of us, "For you was once darkness, but now you are light in the Lord" (Ephesians 5:8). I admit that I had a past with much more darkness in it compared to many. As a result of my alcoholism, I was arrested 8 times, had my stomach pumped, have a few physical scars and emotional scars and had numerous accidents. For a number of years, I thoughtlessly endangered many lives as a result of my drunk driving. I was addicted to pornography for years. As a youth I stole many things. I was a thief. I was a very self-centered and selfish person. My purpose is not to put before you a dramatic conversion story but to reveal to you my character flaws which were many. Was I instantly and miraculously delivered from my past after becoming a Christian? No! Although my standing before my heavenly Father was immediate and there was rejoicing in Heaven my character transformation has been slow and accompanied with victories and with setbacks. What was immediate in my conversion was my being justified, my standing before God. This is true of all Christians regardless of their past. But the sanctifying process is like our fingerprints, it is different for each and every one of us. Though I, like Peter, overwhelmed by my sinfulness on many occasions, felt unworthy to come into the Lord's presence even after becoming a Christian, I am thankful for God's promises concerning those who are born again. Here are just a few. "Being confident of this, that He who began a good work in you will carry it on to completion until the day of Christ Jesus" (Philippians 1:6). "He will keep you strong to the end, so you will be blameless on the day of our Lord Jesus Christ. God, who has called you into fellowship with His Son Jesus Christ our Lord, is faithful" (I Corinthians 1:8-9). "I give them eternal life, and they shall never perish; no one can snatch them out of my hand. My Father, who has given them to me, is greater than all; no one can snatch them out of my Father's hand. I and the Father are one." (John 10:28-30). No, my Christian walk has not been flawless. The doctrine of justification and sanctification are very important but there is another doctrine that should help us keep our eyes fixed on Jesus. It is the doctrine of glorification, when all of us who have been born again will enter into the very presence of God in His heavenly kingdom! The day we will be reunited with those we love who have gone before us. What a day of rejoicing that will be! Every Christian has a testimony. It does not have to be sensational. "That if you confess with mouth, "Jesus is Lord," and believe in your heart that God raised him from the dead, you will be saved. For it is with your heart that you believe and are justified, and it with your mouth that you confess and are saved." (Romans 10:9-10).